[illegible]

snow, the most severe frosts of the century and wide-spread floods kept anglers away for most of January.

The 1982-83 season had yet to open when this edition of ANGLER'S MAIL ANNUAL went to press but anglers, forever optimists, were clearly expecting a super season with experts predicting the fall of several important records. Perhaps it is closer to reality to suggest that by the very nature of their sport, anglers soldier on in hope and expectation. When the fish do actually turn up on cue, and up to those expectations, the headlines seem to get that much bigger and to sound that much more surprised!

I hope you enjoy the mixture prepared for this eleventh edition of the Annual. Ingredients are as popularly prescribed and include a blend of articles previously published in Angler's Mail weekly and, here, adapted or condensed for permanent book form, plus a range of articles specially commissioned.

The intention is unchanged in my wish to include something of interest to any angler, no matter what branch of the sport is the personal favourite, and for sale at a price within reach of all.

My thanks, as always, to colleagues on Angler's Mail, and to writers, photographers and artists, for their skilful help in preparation.

JOHN INGHAM
Editor

CO

£2.75

MATCH-FISHING SPECIAL

How I've Won £50,000

IVAN MARKS, the Leicester tackle dealer and former England International angling star, has competed at all levels of the sport in his long career and assesses his cash winnings at more than £50,000. In this special feature Ivan takes a frank look over the years in which he became one of the best-known faces in fishing.

MY memory for details is not a strong point. I soon forget match-winning weights and facts but I like to think that's because I don't look back very often! I prefer to look forward to what is going to happen.

But some things I do recall very clearly. When I was 10 years old I was helped and encouraged by Phil Coles' father, Alan. He assisted with my fishing and as he was also a greyhound trainer that might help to explain my enthusiasm for gambling!

TOP MARKS!

Alan, and then Eddie Allen, put me on the right road. Eddie was convinced I was different from most other lads he had seen and he backed his judgement by giving me a very great deal of his spare time. He talked me into the Leicester Black Horse club, the outfit which produced most of the Leicester AS National team in those days, and after winning a number of club contests I made it to the Leicester team on the Huntspill in the mid-1950s.

I can't recall my weight. It might have been 2 lb. or 3 lb. but if I failed that day it certainly never registered with me. Soon afterwards I was drawn at the very next peg to Billy Lane in a Coventry match.

He gave me a ticking-off because I called him Mr Lane. He didn't like that and said I should call him Billy. Then he talked about the match and said he thought he could win it. Well, if you can win it, I can come second, I promised myself and that was how we finished with Billy first and me second.

That was on the Great Ouse at Little Paxton and although Billy beat me that day when we both caught roach and skimmers, I was never again too respectful of men at the next pegs.

I once won two matches in one day. First, a Black Horse event at Littleport and then an afternoon Open match in the same area. I was very young and not very big at the time and I recall match organiser Dennis Clarke being surprised that someone so small and young should want to go all the way on the pools to the extent of a full £1. But I did and I won!

I've been winning matches ever since but have never kept a record of any sort. I've got 70 or 80 cups and trophies at home but it sometimes takes me all my time to remember where and how I won them. I suppose I must have won nearly 200 good, sizeable matches, perhaps more, but I've no way of knowing.

There's every chance I shall win more than a few more yet. Eyes are the one crucial factor and my vision is in excellent nick although 45 now and moving into the time when some people do have eye trouble.

But my eyes are good for both long and near sight and my reactions are sharp and I am as dedicated to winning matches as ever I was.

I haven't a clue how much money I've won. I never kept a record and, I must admit, I've not kept much of the money either! I suppose, everything added together, I must have won over £50,000.

The money has been useful but, oddly enough, my real aim is always to finish high up in the league table of money winners. In the last 20 years my worst season produced £1,500; my best—a record at the time—is £7,000.

I've never been out of the top 20 money winners in all that time, winning south, east and west, but never north of Nottingham. Not that I've anything against Yorkshire but there have always been enough big matches nearer home to keep me fully occupied.

I've been highly chuffed about some of my best performances and among those has to be three wins in four years in the Great Ouse Championship.

Anyone who does that needs a chunk of luck at the draw as it's quite remarkable to have had the chance to win three times out of four, considering the contest used to be fished by anything from 500 to 800 anglers at a time.

But there were a number of potentially-winning pegs in that match. Lots of duff ones, too, but at that time it was easier to win a contest at a peg that wasn't quite so good as it was at some of the others.

The oddity about that sequence of wins was that most people preferred not to believe me when I said openly that the real secret of my success was size 20 hooks.

Most scoffed and thought I was covering up some other secret. The other part of that "secret" was my use of 1 lb. breaking strain hooklengths and they wouldn't believe that either!

Makes you think though, doesn't it? How many fish would have been caught in the period immediately after World War II if the anglers had tackled up with small hooks and fine lines?

WOTALOTIVANSGOT! This is the massive array of cups, trophies and medals won by Ivan Marks over his years in match-fishing and he's still winning. Ivan writes every week in Angler's Mail.

Ivan has a soft spot for bream. They have helped him win a string of big competitions, especially on the rivers Ouse and Welland.

These days they use 12 oz bottoms and size 24 barbless hooks and land big fish on them. How many more could they have caught years ago . . . on those days when they thought the fish weren't feeding?

I won the giant Hall AS opens twice in three years and finished second in the year I dipped out! I've won the Middle Level Championship and chalked up wins on all the big rivers but my real love is team fishing. That's the real challenge of fishing, so far as I'm concerned.

My Leicester AS won the National Championship in the last year when it was a weight and not a points aggregate which counted. We beat the "Brummies" on their own patch and I liked that a lot!

We had a marvellous team at that time and with modest pruning it looked as though it might last for years. But that didn't happen. The team fell apart through some people packing up, some getting married and not having so much spare time and others moving away.

We also lost some of the youngsters I had been grooming as replacements and we were never the same after that. Which really explains why I joined the Barnsley Blacks.

I haven't got the time to build a new team almost from scratch. This can't be done quickly so I joined a good team that will offer me a chance of the team fishing I like best.

But for me there's only one team event that is really important above all else, the one that really matters. That's the World Championship.

It was quite a blow to be dropped in 1981 but I want my place back if there's the slightest chance. The greatest honour I could ever hope to win in my lifetime is to be part of an England team win in the World Championship. The individual championship is nothing compared to that. That's not meant to belittle what some very good anglers have already done for England. It's great to see an Englishman do what Dave Thomas did in 1981, so full marks and all credit to him.

But the team event is the one that really counts. Stan Smith, the England team manager, has had four team seconds and a third in the last 10 years but no-one remembers that. It's the team win that remains elusive. To be second is to have failed.

That's my whole philosophy. I took pride in finishing fourth individual in the World Championship in Bulgaria with 24 lb in three hours. That's the biggest weight ever taken by an Englishman in a World Championship so that's a "first" of a sort.

On the following day I finished second in the individual championship with 17 lb in 1½ hours. I enjoyed it but it was a much more relaxed, less important occasion.

The man who has had the biggest influence on my life in recent years is Roy Marlow, my partner in our Leicester tackle shop. I first met Roy when he was just 19 years old. I saw him fishing the Leicester Canal, rated him straight away and wanted him in my Leicester team. He looked good . . . big, strong, capable and young . . . everything was right about him except that he was considering nominating for another team!

But we had a chat and soon changed that. So Roy fished for Leicester AS in the Witham National Championship and finished runner-up to Roy Jarvis. That got him into the England team in the following year for at that time the men who returned the top five weights in the five leading teams made up the England team.

Roy made also his mark there. Fishing in a tributary of the Danube, he finished in individual fourth place and might have done a little better if he hadn't come unstuck from a carp.

After that Roy and I fished together and I suppose it was inevitable we should eventually work together. It was Roy's idea that we should set up a tackle business but that needed a bit of thought at the time. I wasn't too happy working as an engineer but had recently married with more responsibilities than before. Anyway, I thought I might just as well jump into two deep ends at once so I was married and into the business in the same year and I've never looked back since then.

The fact that Roy and shop manager Graham Barry encourage me to fish and let me go even when under pressure in the shop, is wonderful. There are times when I go fishing seven days a week—just like Benny Ashurst— and that's the life for me!

There have been many changes in all the years I've been going fishing. My biggest regret has to be over the deterioration of so many waters where I've enjoyed myself so much in the past. I don't believe some of them will ever again be as good as they once were but, at least, some are improving a little.

I would like to see fishing accorded greater acknowledgement for its value as a worthwhile pastime. Once the politicians get around to realising how important fishing really is to happiness maybe we shall get fish stocks, rivers and fishing taken more seriously.

The greatest advances in fishing techniques in the next 10 years will come inevitably in groundbait and swim-feeding.

We are as good as the French at catching fish but clearly we lag behind over swim-feeding, but once we realise the full value of additives in groundbait we shall make real progress.

Would you like fish and chips without salt and vinegar? Probably not. So don't you think that fish have taste buds, too? Can't they be made more responsive by flavouring their food?

The answer has to be "yes". My groundbait ALWAYS contains an additive of one sort or another. I've not proved anything worth passing on yet but I'm convinced this is where the next major breakthrough will come.

I like being under pressure to achieve things. I need to find out about additives and I need to produce some continuous form to stay in contention for a place in the Barnsley team. They have a squad of 16 and only 12 can fish so that puts the pressure on everyone, which is what contest fishing is all about.

I don't have any real ambition to catch big fish. That aspect of angling has never appealed to me. I prefer to go for the biggest attainable weight of fish within the duration of a fishing match. That's my kind of fishing.

I will never turn up my nose at a 5 lb chub, or a huge bream or two, because they're weight-builders. A 5 lb chub is better than two at 2½ lb but only if you can get it out faster!

I'll go anywhere to fish in a match, provided I'm free to go. I think nothing of driving 100 miles and more on the day and another 100 to get home afterwards.

It's this sort of commitment and enthusiasm that helps keep me competitive. I want to win now just as much as when I first started . . . and that's the essential ingredient for any successful match-fishing career.

Chris Marks, Ivan's young son, is making an early start on his piscatorial path. He landed this bream on Dad's rod at Coombe Abbey lake, near Coventry.

BEACHCASTING SPECIAL

A DAY ON THE BEACH

Related by John Holden

Setting up camp on the shingle, making sure the umbrellas are safely guyed down.

THEY parked the car behind the Martello tower and loaded their rucksacks. Dave picked his way over the icy mud to the seawall and the morning air cut into his lungs as he looked along the miles of shingle beach.

"Tide's almost dead low." he said to Peter. "There are a couple of umbrellas half-a-mile down. Some anglers must have been there all night."

He could make out the water's edge where waves churned big stones at the foot of the shingle bank. The wind quartered in from the north-east, ruffling the sea grasses at his feet. Forecasters had predicted Force 5 and clouds skirting the eastern horizon confirmed a promise of wind towards high tide—perfect for cod.

They set off along the bank, walking by the sea where the stones lay more compact. It was easier walking there but after a mile they stopped for a breather and to pick out their marks now that the sun had lifted. Last time they had fished just past the second notice board on the bird sanctuary.

In past seasons it had marked a deep hole offshore where the tide swirled small fish and crabs to the waiting cod. But autumn storms had changed the seabed, levelling out the gulley and tossing acres of shingle over the muddy bottom.

Peter scanned the tideline. "Looks like a deep patch out there," pointing

Dave's back-cast reached 170 yards out, even allowing 20 yards for wind and bait resistance.

to a gap in the line of breakers. For a hundred yards the water rolled without cresting over. The sea looked little different from the rest, except that the water was oily and heavy. Most anglers would not have noticed the subtle change in the wave pattern and tidal flow.

"Could do worse than try it," Dave suggested. He figured the distance back to the high-water mark at around 150 yards at high tide. "If the wind stays where it is we can get bait out that far. And we're two days off springs so the gear should hold bottom. Might be an 8-ounce job all the same."

They set up camp on the shingle, high up the slope beyond the backwash, where Dave filled two small sacks with stones to hold down the umbrella guy ropes. Peter trenched the umbrella skirts into the beach so that the two canopies formed a long oval barrier against the wind.

The two always fished as a team with two rods each, tackled up and baited to suit the conditions. Some casts were far, others sometimes just in the breakers. This time, with cod and whiting, perhaps a dab, on the cards they fished far out into the offshore gulley.

Dave set up his rods for big fish: single hook paternosters with bait clips and a 4/0 Viking crammed with lugworms.

Peter set up one rod in a similar fashion but tied a two-hook rig to the other leader, baiting the Aberdeen blues with mackerel. "May as well ring the changes," he said. "You can't depend on cod these days. And a lot of flatties were weighed in at last club match."

They cast and rested their rods. Nothing moved: no tide at all, not even crabs to strip the hooks. Dead low water on the East coast does not usually produce many fish, although someone occasionally hooks a big cod in winter or a double-figure bass in late summer. Fishing in this barren spell means knowing that the first trickle of flood can trigger a feeding explosion.

The line from Dave's back-cast shifted in the wind. The swells picked up the slack and swirled it in the backwash, teasing the rod tip up and down. He had cast a long way: even allowing 20 yards for bait resistance and wind his rig was 170 yards out. The line rose slowly from the surf, tightening against the rod and then sagged. "The tide is just starting to make," he observed.

They re-baited and cast again. Dave left the plain sinker on his second rod, cast further than the first rig and a little down stream so that it rolled clear of the other lines.

Peter changed his original plan so that one bait stayed well out and the double paternoster dropped barely 50 yards from the stones. He left ten yards of slack in the big cast so that the making tide would set the grip wires hard in the seabed. On the short cast he gave no slack and the nylon stretched tight and straight between baits and rod tip for even dab bites to show.

Dave's sinker bumped and skidded down tide, anchored and pulled free, drifting slowly inshore. He could tell by the rhythm of the tip, and the angle of the nylon, that his sinker had dragged over a sandbank and into the hole they had seen at low water.

Out to sea there was no longer any indication of a break in the beach contours. He knew that one foot of extra depth can ruin the wave pattern and that it always paid to survey the beach at lowest water, preferably on equinox tides.

"You can walk right past the perfect mark if a few minutes too early or late," he reminded them both.

Peter's rod bounced. "Whiting," he said as he picked up his rod, felt the line pressure on the tip and pulled back. There was no fight at all, just a bit more weight than normal on the retrieve as a whiting tumbled through the surf on to the wet stones.

"This time of year you get to think that once you've hooked a whiting, you've caught the whole lot. They get to be a pain", came Peter's mock grumble.

He looked at the fish, turning it over as winter sun reflected from the oversize eye and pink flanks. He removed the hook and wad of chewed mackerel from the whiting's lip, before tossing the fish back into the sea where it flipped over and sank in the current.

An hour later, and a dozen whiting in the bag, Peter took in his rods. He changed the cod rig for another scaled-down paternoster, baiting both sets with lugworms kept from the day before.

As Peter threaded the small, hard worms on to each blue Aberdeen work, the grey juice ran over his fingers. It stunk . . . the way "flatties" like a lugworm.

The first sinker splashed down 75 yards away, the other only half that. Within five minutes the close-in rod indicated a bite and Peter wound in steadily, neither striking nor giving slack. Two fat dabs skittered from the sea.

He unhooked them and re-baited. "Why don't you change down and get some yourself?" he asked Dave, who ignored the advice. It was a cod or nothing for Dave.

"Look, mate you're not going to get a fish that way," Peter observed as the sun dropped behind the shingle bank, spotlighting the tip of Dave's heavy rod which hadn't moved all day except when a whiting hit his lugworms just after midday.

The tide had come and gone, run and slowed, then picked up on the ebb. Now it ran so fast that tackle bounced 20 yards downstream before the grip wires clawed in and held.

"Just plain stubborn", thought Peter, as he went back to his own rod to wind in another dab. Then he cast and put his rod back in the rest.

Beside him a fixed-spool whirred into action and feet skidded on the shingle.

"Got the gaff?", Dave called. He was thigh-deep in the sea, rod strained over so hard that the line sang. Ninety yards out a big cod shook its head in heavy sullen resistance.

"Last time you did this," Peter joked, "you hauled out a plastic fertiliser bag."

Dave whipped in ten yards of slack as the big cod rode the undertow. "Not this time," he shouted gleefully, wading downstream in pace with the running fish.

Dave's cod safely on the beach, alongside a smaller specimen hooked later in the session.

A DAY OVER THE DEEPS

If this fictional account of the Nag's Head Sea Angling Club and its problems seems familiar to veteran clubmen it's because their trials and tribulations (and occasional disasters) can be typical of some plans for a Day Over The Deeps . . . if the organisation of the trip is not well planned and responsibilities properly shared instead of resting on the shoulders of one person.

Plymouth writer RUSS SYMONS has drawn on his deep knowledge of sea fishing clubs and their ways in preparing this informative tale which, in narrative style, sets out a sound working plan for a successful deep-sea charter trip.

by
RUSS
SYMONS

A successful deep-sea charter trip depends on good organisation, friendly co-operation and, eventually, the chance of a good catch. When the day goes well, the fight between hunter and quarry will produce pictures like this.

"ORDER, order . . . come on lads, let's have some order for this meeting, or we will be here all night!"

The big, florid-faced chairman shouted around the room at the Nag's Head bar and the hubbub died down.

In more conciliatory tones, the chairman continued: "We all seem agreed that our last boat trip down West was a disaster. What we have to do is to learn from those mistakes, and make sure we don't make them again. Young Willie, your new club secretary, has a few ideas he wants to put to this meeting for your approval".

The members of Nag's Head Sea Anglers knew Willie Jones as a keen committed angler—and that he was timid about speaking to a full meeting for the first time, so they settled back with their beer and tobacco, ready to give him tolerant attention.

"I propose we spread the load, so that one man is responsible for transport, another for accommodation, with me looking after the booking of boat and bait".

"That way we will all know what the others are doing, so that we have an overlap of responsibility and one man falling sick will not mean the whole plan collapses like a pack of cards".

The meeting drew rapidly to a conclusion as two members volunteered to help Willie with the organising and an approximate date was set for the club's next trip. Then down the rickety stairs they rushed to get in at least another pint before closing time.

Next evening, Willie consulted his tide tables and 'phoned Fred, the club's favourite boatman, and asked for a booking.

Fred agreed the date, asked for confirmation as soon as possible, accompanied by a deposit, and reminded Willie to telephone on the night before in case the weather looked unfavourable.

"There's no point in travelling all the way down here for me to tell you that the trip is cancelled" warned Fred.

Next, a motor coach was organised and accommodation negotiated with a small hotel glad of the out-of-season trade. The hotel even offered freezer space for anglers to freeze their catch before setting off on the long journey home.

Willie checked with Skipper Fred and confirmed that no fish limit would apply—all that was caught they could take.

Fred worked a very simple system. On full boat charters, paying the full fee, there was no fish limit, On part-bookings, when he went to sea with only a few anglers, he operated a two-fish limit so that the few stone of fish he gained helped to pay the costs of the day out.

In the days before the trip, club members watched TV weather charts, praying for a good high-pressure system to settle for a few days. But on the evening before their departure the weather position was still inconclusive and the "go" or "no go" depended on the skipper's say-so.

"It's OK", said Fred. "But make sure your lads bring some proper foul-weather gear", he advised.

A few telephone calls reminded members to check tackle, waterproofs, boots, food and seasick pills and to lay it all out so that it was almost impossible to forget anything . . . and get early to bed ready for a 3 a.m. start, a day out fishing, followed by a good meal, a few beers, a good night's sleep in the hotel and a leisurely ride home on the Sunday morning.

At 3 a.m. they gathered outside the Nag's Head, their gear was packed into the coach and ten minutes later they were on the motorway heading west.

The coach made good time and arrived over an hour early with the members keyed up and ready to go. So when one of the old hands suggested going over the quay to Lil's place for a bite of breakfast there was complete and immediate agreement.

Fortified by bacon and eggs and a pot of sweet barklike tea, they embarked an hour later on the "Lazy Lobber", which had been converted to angling use by the simple expedient of removing winches and assorted deck clutter so that behind the wheel-

These two 40 lb.-plus ling scored a rare double, even for Plymouth old hands who are more accustomed than most to heavyweight catches. The fish took baited pirks from Ray Parsons' boat, "Sunlit Waters", in late November.

house was a clear and uncluttered deck space.

Skipper Fred was in a good mood. The weather which had seemed threatening the day before was nowhere to be seen. It was a bright crisp November morning with a bit of sea running but no problem for the "Lazy Lobber". The crew of lads he had on board were a good crowd and although he had told them there was no fish limit he knew they would take only what they required for their own immediate needs. They would probably leave a few stone of fish for him so he had made sure there was ice in the fish pound.

Three hours later the engine tone muted as Fred closed the throttles and immediately there was an air of expectancy as the old hands crowded the cabin door for a glimpse of the echo-sounder as Fred swung the wheel to move the boat precisely over the Decca co-ordinates.

A deep wreck presented a vague picture on the graph paper but there was nothing vague about the huge cloud of fish swarming in the turbulent water above the wreckage.

Fred knew more or less how the boat was going to drift as he had fished this sort of tide and wind before. So he moved up a few points on his Decca set and put the boat into neutral.

"OK, lads, over you go", he shouted. Immediately, most of the anglers lowered their long traces over the side, sending their redgills and Eddystone eels down into the depths.

But Willie and a couple of the others had fished with Fred before. They knew that as soon as the fish showed on the sounder trace he would come through the cabin door with a big Hardy Rod and 6/0 Senator red-plate reel, kitted up with a heavy

A small pollack comes aboard after taking a large, glinting pirk.

pirk at the end and half-a-dozen eels paternostered off his 50 lb. breaking strain monofilament.

Killer gear he called it, and they knew how much Fred depended on those extra few stone of fish to pay for the diesel on these deep-water trips.

Sure enough, Fred appeared in the cabin door, favourite rod in hand, "Come on, you lot. Do I have to show you how to catch 'em again?" he teased.

This was the moment the old hands had been waiting for and over the side went their heavy pirks, plummeting down into the thick cluster of fish showing on the echo-sounder.

Fred's rod was soon bending into fish as he urged them to watch out for the wreck, his eye on those bouncing a squid or fish bait along the bottom seeking a cod or ling.

Willie's rod bent until the tip eye touched the tops of the passing waves, the rod butt seated firmly in his belly pad as he battled silently with a coalfish which had hit his pirk like an express train.

The others soon had their fish on the surface, walking their lines back up the boat to keep them clear of Willie's taut struggle.

Two of the most experienced picked up gaffs and moved to Willie's side ready to assist but Fred picked up his huge landing net.

"One of you get to the stern in case it comes off but we will get it in the net so that it won't lose any weight", he instructed.

Fred dipped the net, bringing it up over the tail of the fish so that it was engulfed before it knew what had happened.

Willie couldn't believe his eyes. The coalfish was a superb specimen.

"Twenty-five pounds if it's an ounce", pronounced Fred, shaking the fish out of the net. "Get the hook out and put it down in the ice. Then it won't lose any weight, before we weigh-in for an award."

The day passed quickly as the Nag's Head members caught ling, plus a few pollack for those who persisted with pirks and eels.

At 3.30 p.m. Fred shouted "Come up, lads, that's it" and the "Lazy Lobber" pointed her bows North and headed home as the anglers stowed their gear, got the fish on deck and set to work cleaning and filleting those they wanted to take home.

When the boat moored up alongside the dock, Willie went into the cabin and paid Fred for the day's charter, thanking him for superb sport and, at the same time, making a provisional booking for next trip.

MY WORLD

WE booked two days sharking out of Padstow on the Lady Jane II, skippered by Ray Provis. On the Thursday morning, the first day, we discussed how great it would be to boat a nice-sized shark but by that evening, my husband Jorge, 11 year-old stepson Rupert, and myself, decided not to do any more talking about sharks, thinking it would be unlucky for our second trip on Saturday as we suffered a blank day at Crackington Haven.

Saturday came and we set out from Padstow on a lovely morning and as the weather was so good, decided to go further along the coast to Hartland Point, arriving at midday after a stop on the way to catch fresh mackerel for bait.

Jorge got our shark outfits ready. Mine was an 80 lb class Hardy boat rod and Fin-Nor Regal lever drag reel loaded with 450 yards of 80 lb Ande monofilament.

Ray put out the rubby-dubby bags and threaded the 10/0 hooks with double mackerel baits with the first mackerel up the trace and the second, filleted, hanging from the gape of the hook.

Jorge put out his 50 lb class line first—we had already decided after studying the record lists that I would fish the 80 lb and he with the 50 lb. He had a take straight away and soon boated a 75 lb porbeagle. The fish had taken the bait deep so we couldn't release it as we have done with small sharks on previous trips.

Then Jorge put out both outfits again and bang!—my line went. I immediately put on a kidney harness and clipped it on my reel as Jorge helped me don a butt pad.

The fish had taken the bait properly and didn't mess about as I've known them to do. A nice long run, and then it stopped. As it began a second run, I "threw" the lever on the reel and leaned back on the rod to set the hook. Off it went again and we knew we had a good fish, putting up a good fight and taking plenty of line.

I sat on the engine cover, braced my feet on the side of the boat and began to lean back to give the shark some stick and try to recover the line. I felt very uncomfortable as the butt pad began to dig into my stomach.

We saw the shark come to the top twice just under the surface, but each time it ran again and it was back to work. But the third time I got the swivel to the rod tip and Ray grabbed the trace and gaffed the fish in the head while Jorge put in the second flying gaff near the tail.

I stood ready with the reel drag slackened in case the fish should jump off the gaffs and run again but this time there was no trouble. The tail rope went on and the shark was mine.

Ray and Jorge considered it to be a good fish and I asked them to guess the weight, hoping it would go over the 187 lb mark, which was the women's 80 lb class British record. They estimated it to be 150-200 lb and I had to keep calm and not keep wondering what it might weigh—which was very difficult with the shark lying in front of me all day!

Jorge started to fish again But I told him I was satisfied with my catch! As soon as he put his line out he had another shark of 133 lb. Then he threaded on another bait, put his line out once more, and again had an immediate run. This time it was a 140-pounder.

We were amazed. I have been sharking for three years and Jorge for 10 but we have never had four sharks between us in an afternoon in 2½ hours.

Back at the "Lady Jane's" mooring, Ray got out the scales and weighed my fish. The scales read up to 200 lb but the shark was over that.

Now things began to happen. I knew the women's 80 lb class world record was 230 lb, and wondered if my shark could possibly beat it. Ray radio'd to John Watts on shore—John owns the "Lady Jane" and is the official weighmaster in Rock—to say it was a British record and might be a world beater. Could John please bring bigger scales?

John arrived within half an hour to weigh the fish. I wanted to look but didn't! The weight was 240 lb on the boat, which gave us another world record as Jorge has the all-tackle porbeagle world title with a 465 pounder, a record he's held for five years.

We were delighted and I was stunned. Then we had to get the shark on land to weigh it officially for the IGFA world record claim. John radio'd to Padstow across the estuary and they stood ready with a crane to weigh the fish on land where it registered 236 lb, beating the old record, held for 16 years out of Montauk Point, New York, by 6 lb.

SUCCESS STORY

RECORD SHARK

LOG

Date: August 11, 1981
Catch: 236 lb porbeagle shark, IGFA World Record for women's 80 lb line class.
Location: one mile off Hartland Point, Padstow, Cornwall.
Captor: Marie Potier of Holland Park, West London.

by
Marie
Potier

Shark hunter Marie Potier with the 236 lb. porbeagle which gave her a woman's world title under International Game Fishing Association line-class rules. Her husband, Jorge Potier holds the all-tackle porbeagle title with a 465-pounder.

STILLWATER FISHING

Jim Gibbinson, one of Britain's most knowledgeable and successful anglers, is convinced that stillwaters represent anglers' best hopes for the future of coarse fishing. This stems from his belief that in 20 or 30 years' time there will be little river fishing of any consequence left in this country. Jim's series on Stillwater Fishing attracted considerable attention when first published in Angler's Mail over several issues in 1981. This special selection from the series will help newcomers and old hands alike to get more from their sport at gravel pits and lakes.

GETTING TO GRIPS WITH GRAVEL PITS

Various types of water result from excavation but gravel pits are probably the most common and certainly the most important from an angling point of view.

Making sense of these pits means needing to know a little about how they are dug but first I'd like to establish some terminology because there is little point in talking about "bars" or "shelves" unless the expressions mean the same to you as they do to me:

BAR: an underwater ridge created by the dumping of soil.

GULLY OR TROUGH: a long depression in the lake-bed created during excavation.

SHELF: an area of rapid depth change, possibly the side of a bar.

PLATEAU: a large area of fairly constant depth.

Most lakes and ponds have shallow margins and a deeper centre, except for ornamental lakes which frequently have their deepest water at the dam end. Gravel pits have a corrugated configuration due to the nature of their excavation. This is because there is invariably a layer of topsoil to remove before the gravel layer is reached.

This spoil is dumped alongside the dragline or excavator, creating ridges that will become islands or submerged bars when the pit is eventually flooded. Even if the bars can't be seen, their direction and spacing can usually be gauged from points and promontories along the shoreline.

Occasionally, having dug the length of the pit, the drag will work across and instead of the usual corrugated bottom a much more complex egg-box conformation results.

In the 1940's and early 1950's pits were usually back-filled, often with fly-ash from power stations. Since the late 50's the tendency has been for them to be kept open and they've been adopted by boaters and naturalists as well as by anglers.

The significance of this, in biological terms is that most pits are very young environments, as demonstrated in a study undertaken by Dr. Ann Powell of City of London Polytechnic in conjunction with Leisure Sport.

Silt eventually collects in gullies between the ridges and rooted weeds become established. Until that happens the only weed of any consequence may be filamentous algae. I don't think margin plants like reeds and rushes become established until the banks cave in and produce topsoil deposits around the edges.

Lack of weed results in a shortage of good spawning and nursery areas which is why many pits appear to be grossly understocked. As a pit matures and weeds become established so spawning and fry-survival improve and the pit becomes capable of supporting a larger population.

When this stage is reached, recruitment will occur naturally and we cannot speed the process by tipping vast quantities of fish in the pit. Few angling clubs seem to be able to grasp this simple fact and countless thousands of pounds have been spent on futile stocking operations.

A typical gravel pit has an undulating bottom and an indented shoreline. Another physical characteristic shared by most pits is that they are relatively shallow, which is at variance with popular folklore which holds that pits are deep and mysterious.

I've fished very many of them over the years and have "pinged" a good number with an echo-sounder, and know of only three with substantial areas deeper than about 20ft. Many have an average depth of less than 10ft.

Knowing how pits are dug, and something of their physical make-up, means we are in a better position to make sense of fish movements within them.

The angler who sits in a pitch chosen because it takes his fancy doesn't really have much chance of doing well. He may be casting his bait to the top of a ridge—where it may lie in no more than a foot of water—or to the bottom of a 15 ft. gully.

Neat and tidy rules about fishing into the wind are not enough to follow for 30 yards out there may be a bar running parallel to the bank. That bar gets the full benefit of the wind and as far as the fish are concerned it is the downwind "bank". Behind this natural breakwater the water may be lifeless and possibly fishless.

So the first thing that needs to be done is some very careful work with a plummet, not just in a handful of pitches but over the whole pit. Only when an angler has a clear mental picture of the pit bottom with all its ridges and depressions can he hope to be consistently successful.

I am willing to bet that the vast majority of specimen pike, tench and carp captured in this country are taken from gravel pits. I'd also bet that more anglers have more blank days in pits than in any other type of water. Which leads us to the fundamental truth that pits can produce colossal fish but do so very grudgingly.

OF THE VARIOUS TYPES OF WATER RESULTING FROM EXCAVATION GRAVEL PITS ARE PROBABLY THE COMMONEST
ANATOMY OF A GRAVEL PIT
ISLAND
PLATEAU
BAR
SHELF
GULLY
MANY PITS HAVE AN AVERAGE DEPTH OF LESS THAN 10 FEET
EVEN IF THE BARS CAN'T BE SEEN THEIR DIRECTION AND SPACING CAN USUALLY BE GAUGED FROM POINTS AND PROMONTORIES ALONG THE SHORELINE
BAR
BAR
BAR
THESE RIDGES (BARS) CREATED BY THE EXCAVATOR WHEN THE PIT WAS DUG SOMETIMES HAVE A MORE COMPLEX PATTERN
Tony Whieldon
THE ANGLER WHO SITS IN A PITCH THAT TAKES HIS FANCY DOESNT REALLY HAVE MUCH CHANCE OF DOING WELL
HE MAY BE CASTING HIS BAIT TO THE TOP OF A RIDGE WHERE IT MIGHT LIE IN NO MORE THAN A FOOT OF WATER, OR TO THE BOTTOM OF A FIFTEEN FOOT GULLY.....
....SO THE FIRST THING THAT NEEDS TO BE DONE IS SOME VERY CAREFUL WORK WITH A PLUMMET – OVER THE WHOLE PIT
ONLY WHEN THE ANGLER HAS A CLEAR MENTAL PICTURE OF THE PIT BOTTOM WITH ALL ITS RIDGES AND DEPRESSIONS CAN HE HOPE TO BE CONSISTENTLY SUCCESSFUL.

STILLWATER FISHING

TRACKING DOWN CARP

CARP are bank-huggers by nature and in a lightly-fished water where they haven't been scared out of the habit they will spend a lot of time patrolling the margins. But most of our carp waters are so hard-fished that only occasionally do the carp come close-in. Even so, the instinct remains and can be exploited if we can find stretches or bank that are quiet and undisturbed—in a word, islands.

Bait tucked tight against islands will pick up lots of fish, even if there is only a foot or two of water. Carp like overhanging cover, particularly trees and bushes which touch or actually penetrate the surface, so an island combined with over-hanging vegetation is almost certainly a carp-holding area.

Their liking for shallow water is well known, sometimes moving into water barely deep enough to cover them, particularly early in the morning.

PLATEAU

The shallow inflow end of an artificial estate lake or a plateau in a gravel pit with anything over 18 in. of water will almost certainly hold carp until well after sunrise if the morning is bright, warm and still. As the morning wears on they may move into deeper water and if a breeze springs up they'll probably respond to it.

Weedbeds are also reliable holding-area. Most mature lakes and gravel pits will have well established areas of weed unless excessive eutrophication has made the water too coloured for rooted weeds to survive.

Weeds which create a "roof", particularly of lilies and floating pondweed *(Potamogeton natans)*, generally hold a few carp. Emergent plants like reeds also do. Sometimes, you'll see fish basking in areas of this sort and despite their lack of activity they will frequently take small, floating baits.

Don't cast the bait directly at a fish or it will spook and either dash off or slowly sink from view. It is better gently to position the bait in a suitable clearing and wait. If they want it, they'll find it.

Occasionally you will not see the fish itself, but will first notice movements of the reeds or lilies. Reeds may shake violently as if a dog was charging through them, and lilies sometimes skate across the surface and submerge. At other times the movements are much more subtle when a reed stem may gently twitch or give a barely perceptible half-roll, or the lily leaf may emit a few concentric rings.

The gentle movements are usually caused by fish swimming deep where the stems are well spread out. More violent movements are the result of fish swimming fairly near the surface where the stems have branched and there is less room.

Men who revolutionised carp fishing in the early 1950's noticed that bubbling frequently accompanied feeding but often found these fish very difficult to catch, leading to the term "indifferent bubbler".

A lot depends on which water is being fished. In some, bubblers are quite easy to tempt. In others they are very contrary indeed. Perhaps the early carp catchers had more than their share of the contrary varieties and gained the impression that bubblers were more difficult than they really are.

My first encounter with bubblers was in a small park lake where my brother Rick and I fished early mornings on our summer holidays from school. This was a long time ago when we were barely out of short trousers and we fished with float tackle with small worms for bait.

We looked for clusters of bubbles, overcast by a couple of yards and gently draw the bait back until it was as close to the fish as we could get it. I'm not claiming that "bubble chasing", as we called it, set the world on fire, but we caught carp fairly consistently topped by an 18 lb. leather for Rick.

Carp bubbles are quite unlike tench needle-bubbles, being large and fewer in number. Sometimes, they come up in clusters, occasionally accompanied by a mud cloud and bits of bottom debris. This sort of bubbles is a real head-down tail-up preoccupied fish.

More often, the bubbles are scattered over quite a wide area indicating that several fish are on the "prod" and they will come to the surface both individually and in groups of four or five.

CATAPULT

When fish are on the move like this it pays to fish the general area instead of casting to individuals. A small worm or bunch of maggots on float tackle or light leger is a tactic as good as any and it pays to catapult a few bait samples in the vicinity.

I usually use maggots or worms for bubblers but particle baits work well, so do small paste baits. I've rarely had much success with big paste baits in these circumstances.

Thus far I have been concerned about what might be called "blind" location, when we rely on what we know about carp behaviour and their response to physical factors like wind and sunshine. But remember that carp are probably the easiest of all fish to locate by direct observation. Their tendency to roll, leap, cruise, bow-wave and indulge in similar extrovert activities is the most reliable give-away of all.

CARP, BY NATURE, ARE BANK-HUGGERS. IN A LIGHTLY FISHED WATER THEY'LL SPEND A LOT OF TIME PATROLLING THE MARGINS
IN HARD FISHED WATERS IT IS DIFFICULT TO FIND A STRETCH OF UNDISTURBED BANK. ISLANDS ARE THE ANSWER HERE
CARP LIKE OVERHANGING COVER. COMBINE AN ISLAND WITH OVERHANGING VEGETATION AND YOU'VE GOT AN ALMOST CERTAIN CARP HOLDING AREA.
THEY'LL SOMETIMES MOVE INTO WATER BARELY DEEP ENOUGH TO COVER THEM, PARTICULARLY EARLY IN THE MORNING
WEEDBEDS ARE RELIABLE HOLDING AREAS AND WEEDS THAT CREATE A ROOF (LILIES AND FLOATING PONDWEED) GENERALLY HOLD A FEW CARP.
Tony Whieldon
SOMETIMES YOU'LL SEE FISH BASKING IN REEDS
THESE FISH WILL FREQUENTLY TAKE A SMALL FLOATING BAIT IF IT IS GENTLY POSITIONED IN A SUITABLE CLEARING
OCCASIONALLY YOU'LL NOT SEE THE FISH ITSELF, YOU'LL SEE MOVEMENTS OF THE REEDS OR LILIES INSTEAD
CARP BUBBLES ARE LARGER THAN TENCH BUBBLES AND FEWER IN NUMBER
OFTEN ACCOMPANIED BY A MUD CLOUD AND BITS OF BOTTOM DEBRIS
A SMALL WORM OR A BUNCH OF MAGGOTS ON FLOAT OR LIGHT LEGER TACKLE WILL SCORE WITH THESE BUBBLERS

STILLWATER FISHING

CARP AT A DISTANCE

FOR consistent success the carp angler needs to have a wide range of methods in his repertoire. Some modern carp-men lack this all-round ability, doing all or most of their fishing in one water. They fish mechanically and, in consequence, become one-method anglers.

But there is no best method. An approach that works well on one water may be a dead loss on another. That is why I am setting out in detail some of the specialised techniques in use.

Where bankside disturbance, or the existence of distant feeding areas result in carp habitually being found a long way out, we need to devise effective ways of fishing at long-range.

The term "long range" means different things to different people, but for our purposes let's assume that anything over 60 yards falls into the category. Obviously, the physical problems are likely to be magnified as the range is extended and distances in excess of 100 yards means entering a very specialised area. Few anglers can fish effectively at that range—most can't cast that far!

COMPROMISE

The best rod for long-range fishing is a fast-taper model with a test-curve of between 2-3 lb. Some anglers prefer rods of 12 ft.-plus, but after a lot of experiment I reckon 11 ft. is a good compromise. Line should be as fine as is practical and for most of my long-range fishing I use 6 or 7 lb test.

If the combined weight of lead and bait exceeds 1½ oz., a shock-leader is necessary or snap-offs will occur when casting. A leader of 11 lb. test is about right. I secure this to a loop tied in the end of my main line, the loop being formed with a special knot called the Bimini-twist. It is the only knot I know that is stronger than the line to which it is tied.

I'm not a fan of ultra-fine, prestretched lines, having found them unreliable and quite unrealistically rated for breaking-strain. I use an inexpensive German perlon that is reliable, tough and has excellent abrasion resistance—an important factor when there are intervening gravel bars over which fish have to be drawn.

DISTANCE

In some waters carp are quite happy to take golf-ball size paste baits, in which case the required distance may be achieved without the use of any lead. Generally, though, there is a tendency these days to use much smaller baits, something between hazelnut and walnut size. In this case extra weight will be needed, 1½ to 2 oz. bomb leads being usual.

A running paternoster is probably the best terminal tackle but remember that if a shock-leader is used the hook-link needs to be no heavier than the main line for it doesn't take the full stress of casting. The lead-link however, needs to be as strong as the shock-leader.

Long casting is made easier if paste baits are frozen and taken to the water in a vacuum flask. If they are used in their soft state a tiny roll of blotting paper should be placed under the bend of the hook and another pushed down the hole where the line comes away. This prevents the bait flying off. Modern "boilies" withstand casting very well.

Prior to casting, the spool should have a few drops of diluted washing-up liquid dripped on to it which will ensure that the line doesn't belly in a cross-wind.

If a carp runs with the bait you can use any of the standard open-spool methods of bite detection, including silver paper or plastic cylinders. But if runs are a rarity you'll have to fish with a closed bale-arm, using a bobbin indicator between butt and second ring.

Some anglers fish with a very short drop and strike at any positive movement. I don't have that sort of concentration so my rods are mounted fairly high with a long drop of two feet or so. If a runner takes the bait I have time to get to the rod. If, on the other hand, I get only a twitch or a short lift I wind up the bobbin so it is only six inches below the rod.

Sometimes I hold the rod and wait for a further movement of the indicator, or I may stand with my hand cupped a couple of inches above the rod handle, read to gather it up and strike all in one movement. This is known among my friends as "'aving an 'ovver"!

PENETRATION

When the strike is made it should be hard. You will not break on the strike when fishing at long range, even with a powerful rod and light line. Penetration is facilitated if the hook is honed to razor sharpness and the barb reduced with a file.

It pays to scatter a few bait samples in the area being fished—four or five to each hookbait is about right and these should be replenished if bites suggest they may have been taken. A catapult is essential for this, the best sort are those made in the USA for vermin control—characterised by special tubular elastic and a wrist support. Maggot and groundbait catapults are useless for this sort of work.

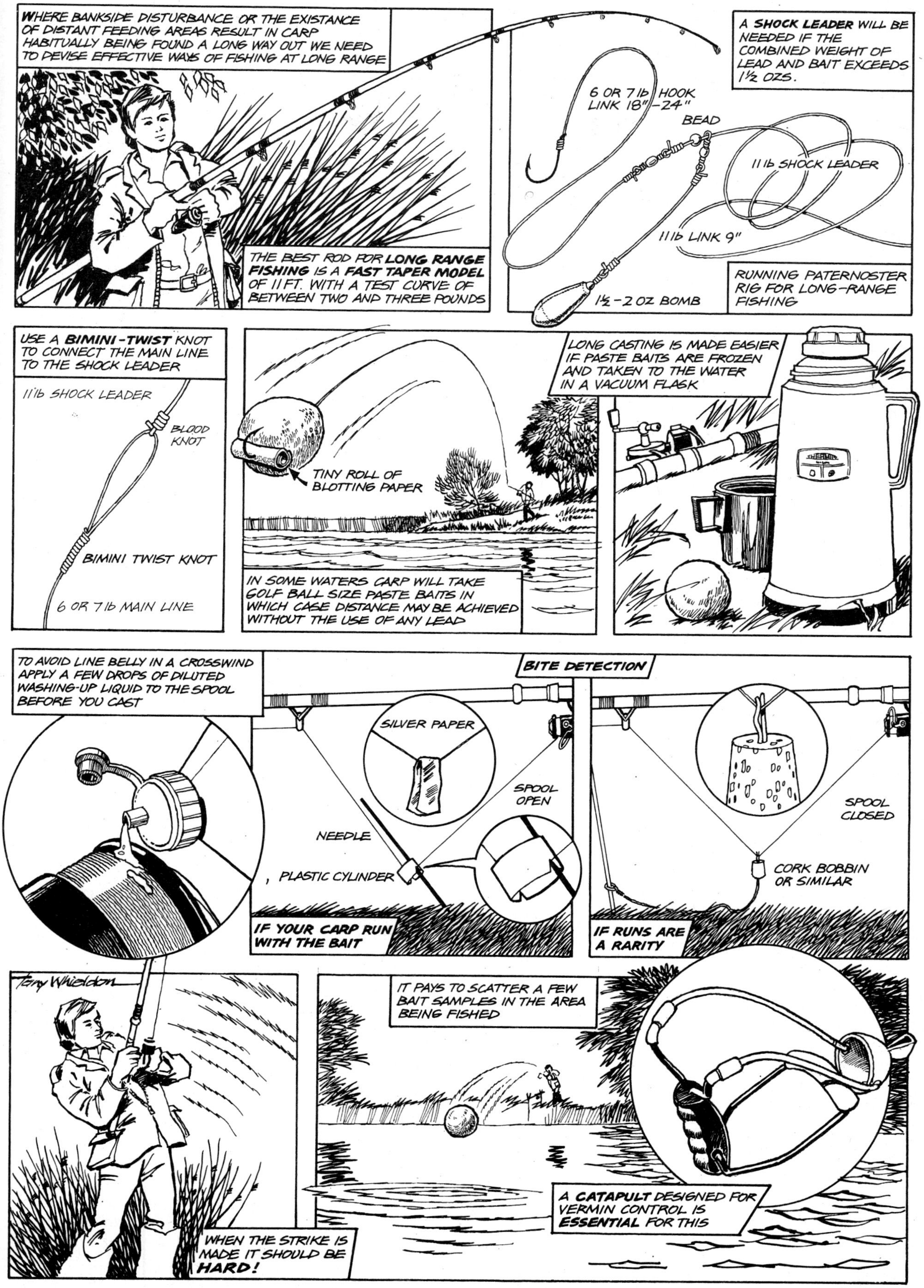

WHERE BANKSIDE DISTURBANCE OR THE EXISTANCE OF DISTANT FEEDING AREAS RESULT IN CARP HABITUALLY BEING FOUND A LONG WAY OUT WE NEED TO DEVISE EFFECTIVE WAYS OF FISHING AT LONG RANGE
THE BEST ROD FOR LONG RANGE FISHING IS A FAST TAPER MODEL OF 11 FT. WITH A TEST CURVE OF BETWEEN TWO AND THREE POUNDS
A SHOCK LEADER WILL BE NEEDED IF THE COMBINED WEIGHT OF LEAD AND BAIT EXCEEDS 1½ OZS.
6 OR 7 lb HOOK LINK 18"-24"
BEAD
11 lb SHOCK LEADER
11 lb LINK 9"
1½ - 2 OZ BOMB
RUNNING PATERNOSTER RIG FOR LONG-RANGE FISHING
USE A BIMINI-TWIST KNOT TO CONNECT THE MAIN LINE TO THE SHOCK LEADER
11 lb SHOCK LEADER
BLOOD KNOT
BIMINI TWIST KNOT
6 OR 7 lb MAIN LINE
TINY ROLL OF BLOTTING PAPER
IN SOME WATERS CARP WILL TAKE GOLF BALL SIZE PASTE BAITS IN WHICH CASE DISTANCE MAY BE ACHIEVED WITHOUT THE USE OF ANY LEAD
LONG CASTING IS MADE EASIER IF PASTE BAITS ARE FROZEN AND TAKEN TO THE WATER IN A VACUUM FLASK
TO AVOID LINE BELLY IN A CROSSWIND APPLY A FEW DROPS OF DILUTED WASHING-UP LIQUID TO THE SPOOL BEFORE YOU CAST
BITE DETECTION
SILVER PAPER
SPOOL OPEN
NEEDLE
PLASTIC CYLINDER
IF YOUR CARP RUN WITH THE BAIT
SPOOL CLOSED
CORK BOBBIN OR SIMILAR
IF RUNS ARE A RARITY
Tony Whieldon
WHEN THE STRIKE IS MADE IT SHOULD BE HARD!
IT PAYS TO SCATTER A FEW BAIT SAMPLES IN THE AREA BEING FISHED
A CATAPULT DESIGNED FOR VERMIN CONTROL IS ESSENTIAL FOR THIS

STILLWATER FISHING

Preparing Carp Baits

MOST modern carp fishing is done with paste baits of one kind or another. These range from simple meat-based pastes to the sophisticated high protein (HP) or, as their originator Fred Wilton prefers to call them, high nutritive value (HNV) baits.

Perhaps the most successful of the meat-based pastes is sausage meat. It is rarely used as many carp-men feel it is inferior to other baits currently in use, but I'm not so sure. Sausage meat was astonishingly productive for those of us who used it in the days when it was still on the "secret" list. As word leaked out it became more widely used and eventually over-used with the result that lots of carp learned to avoid it.

That was ten years or more ago and I strongly suspect that anyone who used sausage meat now would find that carp no longer associate it with danger.

As bought, sausage meat isn't suitable for use as bait as it's too soft and needs stiffening with some cereal. Your can use sausage rusk, finely-ground breadcrumbs, crushed Weetabix, ground rice, semolina, proprietary groundbait . . . the list is virtually endless.

The choice of cereal stiffener will influence the final smell of the paste and this can be further modified by the addition of stock-cubes, soup powders, minced liver, yeast extract and seasoning either singly or in combinations. My first choice is fresh bullock's blood and a special spicy seasoning called "Red Rose" which I obtained from a friend in the meat trade. This had the additional advantage of containing sodium sulphide which is a preservative.

I insist on my meat baits being fresh, having had no success at all with sour baits. Some people claimed successes on "high" baits, but I found such baits useless.

The success of sausage meat paste led anglers to experiment with other meat bases, notably cat and dog foods. They worked well, and still do and their preparation is as described for sausage paste.

Another popular bait from the "specials" era is trout pellet paste. They require no additives, being highly attractive to carp as bought. To make the hard pellets into a paste it is merely necessary to dampen them and allow to soften for half-an-hour or so when they can be kneaded and rolled into balls.

Some brands are reluctant to soften in cold water but will do so readily if scalded with boiling water. Alternatively, they may be ground to a fine talc when they will mix easily.

The HP or HNV baits are much more costly than the baits so far described. At one time it was very difficult to acquire the necessary ingredients but now they are readily obtainable through specialist suppliers who advertise in *Angler's Mail*.

Those suppliers also sell pre-packed ready-mixed baits made to proven recipes and some will prepare baits to your own requirements.

For those who fancy DIY bait-making, here is one of Fred Wilton's own recipes: 5 oz casein, 1 oz Casilan, 1 oz lactalbumin, 1 oz gluten, 1 oz soya flour, 1 oz Equivite.

Flavour is added by means of concentrated essence. Fruit flavours like strawberry and pineapple have been extremely successful, as also have some spicy flavours.

Lactalbumin is inordinately expensive and can probably be omitted from the recipe without harm—something like Protoveg or stabilised wheat-germ might be tried in its place.

For details on the use of these baits and information on the thinking behind them I suggest reading the relevant section written by Fred Wilton in *"Carp and the Carp Angler"* by George Sharman.

Some HNV recipes can be mixed with water to make paste but it is more usual to mix with beaten eggs (10 oz. dry mix to six standard eggs being a general guide). Roll into bait-sized balls and boil for 1½ minuts to give them a protective skin. These "boilies", as they are often called, are then relatively immune from the attentions of "skimmer" bream and the nuisance fish.

The best way to boil them is a few at a time in the wire cage of a chip-pan. The water should be brought to the boil before the baits are plunged in and after 1½ minutes tipped on to newspaper to cool and dry. I make mine in huge batches which are kept in the freezer until required.

If an HNV mix is mixed with twice the usual number of eggs and a level teaspoonful of baking powder, put it in a bread-tin and place on the middle shelf of an oven at gas Mk. 2 for two hours. A sponge-like cake will result which makes an excellent floating bait if cut into cubes of appropriate size.

A newcomer to carp fishing may feel bewildered by references to "AA's" or "acids" in bait discussions. These are amino-acids and some carp anglers believe their addition to a bait can evoke a feeding response. I haven't space to debate the pros and cons here so I'll simply state that the vast majority of carp anglers who buy these additives are wasting their money. The casual, ad-hoc addition of random aminos to baits is an utter waste of time.

Various beans, and seeds collectively known as particle baits, are effective in many waters. Among the most successful are chic-peas, black-eyed beans, red kidney beans, maple peas and broad beans. Some can be bought ready-cooked in cans, otherwise it is necessary to buy them in their dried state and cook them yourself.

As a rough guide, dried beans and so forth should be soaked for six hours then brought to the boil and simmered for twenty minutes.

Sweetcorn has had a lot of publicity as a carp bait and there is no denying that an awful lot of carp have fallen to it. But these days it is over-used and, more important, badly used.

I recommend paying serious attention to "natural" baits such as worms, maggots and casters and don't ignore floating crust, pressed crust, flake and luncheon meat. None of these are very "fashionable" but they'll catch a great many carp!

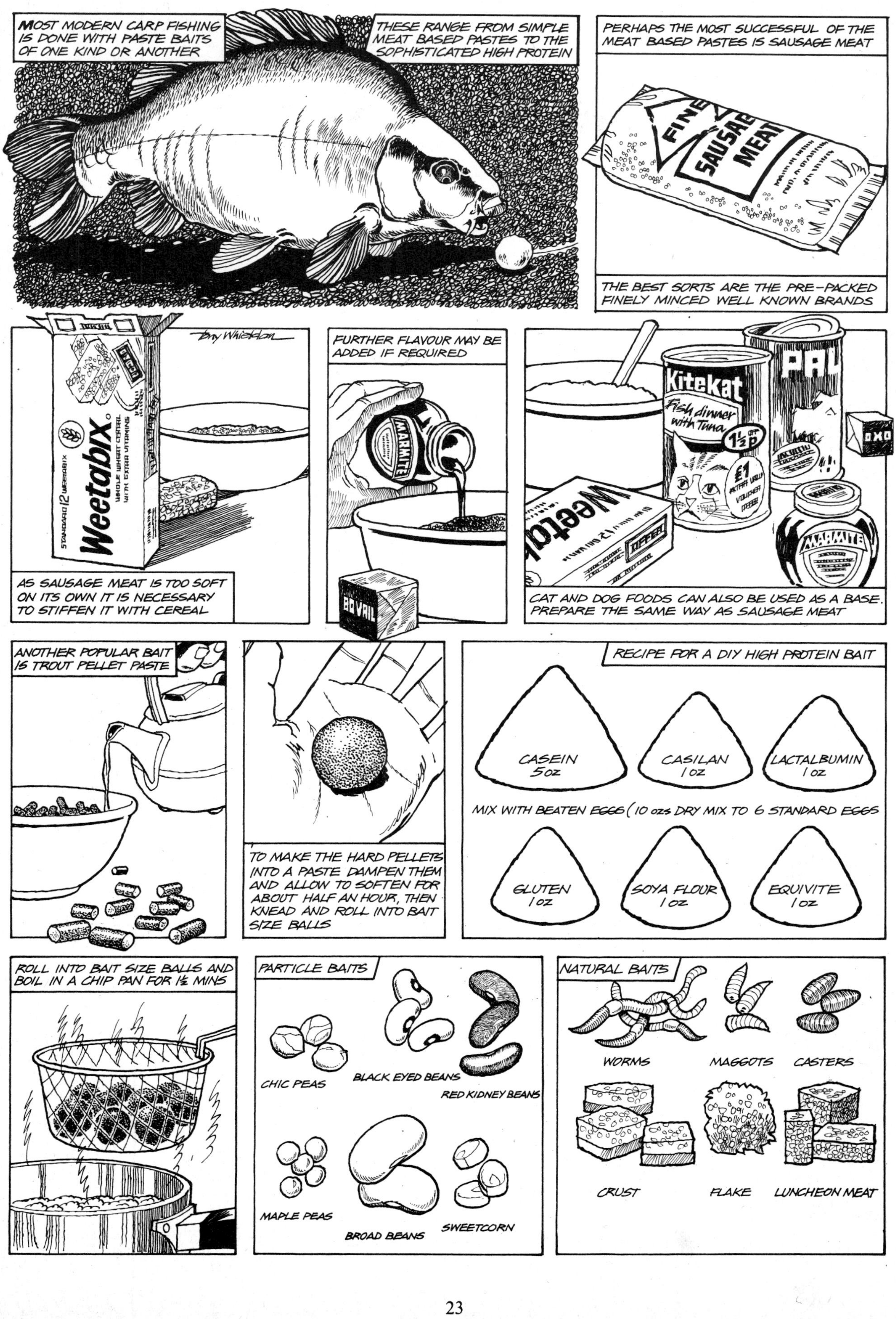
MOST MODERN CARP FISHING IS DONE WITH PASTE BAITS OF ONE KIND OR ANOTHER
THESE RANGE FROM SIMPLE MEAT BASED PASTES TO THE SOPHISTICATED HIGH PROTEIN
PERHAPS THE MOST SUCCESSFUL OF THE MEAT BASED PASTES IS SAUSAGE MEAT
FINE SAUSAGE MEAT
THE BEST SORTS ARE THE PRE-PACKED FINELY MINCED WELL KNOWN BRANDS
Weetabix
AS SAUSAGE MEAT IS TOO SOFT ON ITS OWN IT IS NECESSARY TO STIFFEN IT WITH CEREAL
FURTHER FLAVOUR MAY BE ADDED IF REQUIRED
MARMITE
BOVRIL
Kitekat
Fish dinner with Tuna
OXO
CAT AND DOG FOODS CAN ALSO BE USED AS A BASE. PREPARE THE SAME WAY AS SAUSAGE MEAT
ANOTHER POPULAR BAIT IS TROUT PELLET PASTE
TO MAKE THE HARD PELLETS INTO A PASTE DAMPEN THEM AND ALLOW TO SOFTEN FOR ABOUT HALF AN HOUR, THEN KNEAD AND ROLL INTO BAIT SIZE BALLS
RECIPE FOR A DIY HIGH PROTEIN BAIT
CASEIN 5oz
CASILAN 1oz
LACTALBUMIN 1oz
MIX WITH BEATEN EGGS (10 ozs DRY MIX TO 6 STANDARD EGGS
GLUTEN 1oz
SOYA FLOUR 1oz
EQUIVITE 1oz
ROLL INTO BAIT SIZE BALLS AND BOIL IN A CHIP PAN FOR 1½ MINS
PARTICLE BAITS
CHIC PEAS
BLACK EYED BEANS
RED KIDNEY BEANS
MAPLE PEAS
BROAD BEANS
SWEETCORN
NATURAL BAITS
WORMS
MAGGOTS
CASTERS
CRUST
FLAKE
LUNCHEON MEAT

STILLWATER FISHING

BREAM AT NIGHT

BREAM can be caught in the daytime notably at first light, but there's no denying the best time on many waters is after dark.

Night fishing poses all kinds of problems which don't exist by day, such as accurate casting and feeding. While fish may range a bit farther afield in darkness for their food, it is still an advantage to be able to confine feed time to a tight area and to cast to that area.

If the spot fished is only a gentle under-arm cast from the bank there's no problem but if it's a long way out things can be difficult. To do the job properly it is necessary to make a start in daylight when direction can be established via markers on the skyline, such as trees, rooftops, pylons and so on. Even on the darkest night silhouettes can be seen and the only time the system becomes impractical is in mist or fog.

Spot-on distance casting is not so easy and that's when probably the best tactic is to use a cotton marker on the line. It is a recognised method for night fishing but for the benefit of those not familiar with it I'll describe it in detail.

COTTON MARKER

First cast to the required spot in daylight, then tighten the tackle and tie a piece of cotton to the line level with the butt ring. If the tackle is subsequently overcast it can be retrieved until the cotton marker is realigned when the terminal tackle *must* then be the correct distance from the bank.

Swimfeeder legering ensures that a constant supply of feed is delivered to the chosen spot. Casters and squatts are the most useful feed items and I like to incorporate a highly-scented attractant in the groundbait feeder-plug.

My favourite attractant is made up of roast barley ground small and trout pellets ground to a fine talc. This is mixed with white crumb—I use white after-dark swimfeeder fishing because it holds together better than brown, and that's a necessary attribute when deliberately overcasting a feeder and subsequently pulling it back. A less secure plug would result in the feeder emptying prematurely.

Worms and maggots are excellent bream baits but rather prone to the attentions of mini-eels at night. If "bootlaces" are a problem I opt for flake or pea-sized carp "boilies".

Bream are extremely partial to most "specials" or HNV baits, as any carp angler will testify. Sausage meat paste is particularly effective, as are pastes made from fish-based catfoods.

Bite indication after dark is best provided by some sort of bobbin indicator incorporating a Beta-light. You can make one from a 15 cm (6-inch) length of aquarium plastic air tubing or model aircraft fuel piping. The Beta-light is inserted in the tube and locked in position by a couple of tight fitting beads. A small length of plastic rod or a custom-made air-pipe junction is used as a ferrule, enabling the indicator to be clipped on the line.

The indicator is hung between first and second ring and may be used in isolation or in conjunction with an electric indicator. For brief evening sessions I don't bother with alarms but for all-night stints I regard them as essential.

A ring indicator can be prevented from swinging in the wind by spiking it with a double-pointed knitting kneedle pushed in the ground. This provides virtually friction-free control and is unlikely to "spook" a taking fish.

Swingtips? Frankly, I doubt that their sensitivity is necessary for bream at night and not altogether convinced that it's necessary at any time. If a swingtip is unnecessary it is best dispensed with for it impedes casting and is rather prone to snag the line and tangle in the darkness, especially if rigged with a Beta-light.

I have assumed that leger tackle will be used. It is generally the most effective method but isn't the inevitable choice. Where bream come fairly close to the bank, say up to three rodlengths, floatfishing works fine.

It is possible to use a white-painted float with a torch beam shining on it, but I'm convinced that in some circumstances the light scares fish and makes them wary of feeding. Lights may also annoy other anglers, especially if they are fishing opposite with a powerful beam shining at them.

Much better to use a float with its own inbuilt light. The most popular sort incorporates a Beta-light but if you buy one of these ensure that it has sufficient power. Some of the cheaper models are useless unless fishing almost directly beneath the rod top.

Another type of night-fishing float has a light-emitting diode in the tip which is powered by a hearing-aid mini-battery in the float body. Both types work well but because of their cost they should be fastened very securely to the line. It makes sense to use a hook-link of lower breaking strain than the main line so that the float won't get lost if the hook snags.

KEEP QUIET

The value of fishing close-in depends on many factors, not least the angler's ability to keep quiet! Many species of fish, including bream, will come very close to the margins after dark if they are not frightened, but medium to long-range fishing will generally produce the most consistent results.

A further advantage of fishing at range is that several fish may be taken from the shoal before they realise something is amiss and move-off.

Netting fish in darkness is tricky until you are used to it. Obviously, it pays to have a large landing net—a big, deep carp net is ideal. When the fish is within netting range, crouch low and try to spot where it is swirling. The net should then be gently lifted beneath the disturbance.

If keeping your fish until morning for photographing I recommend a large perforated nylon keep-sack as used by carp anglers. These are far superior to keepnets.

A torch should be carried for the baiting-up, unhooking, and so on. A small penlight is adequate for the purpose.

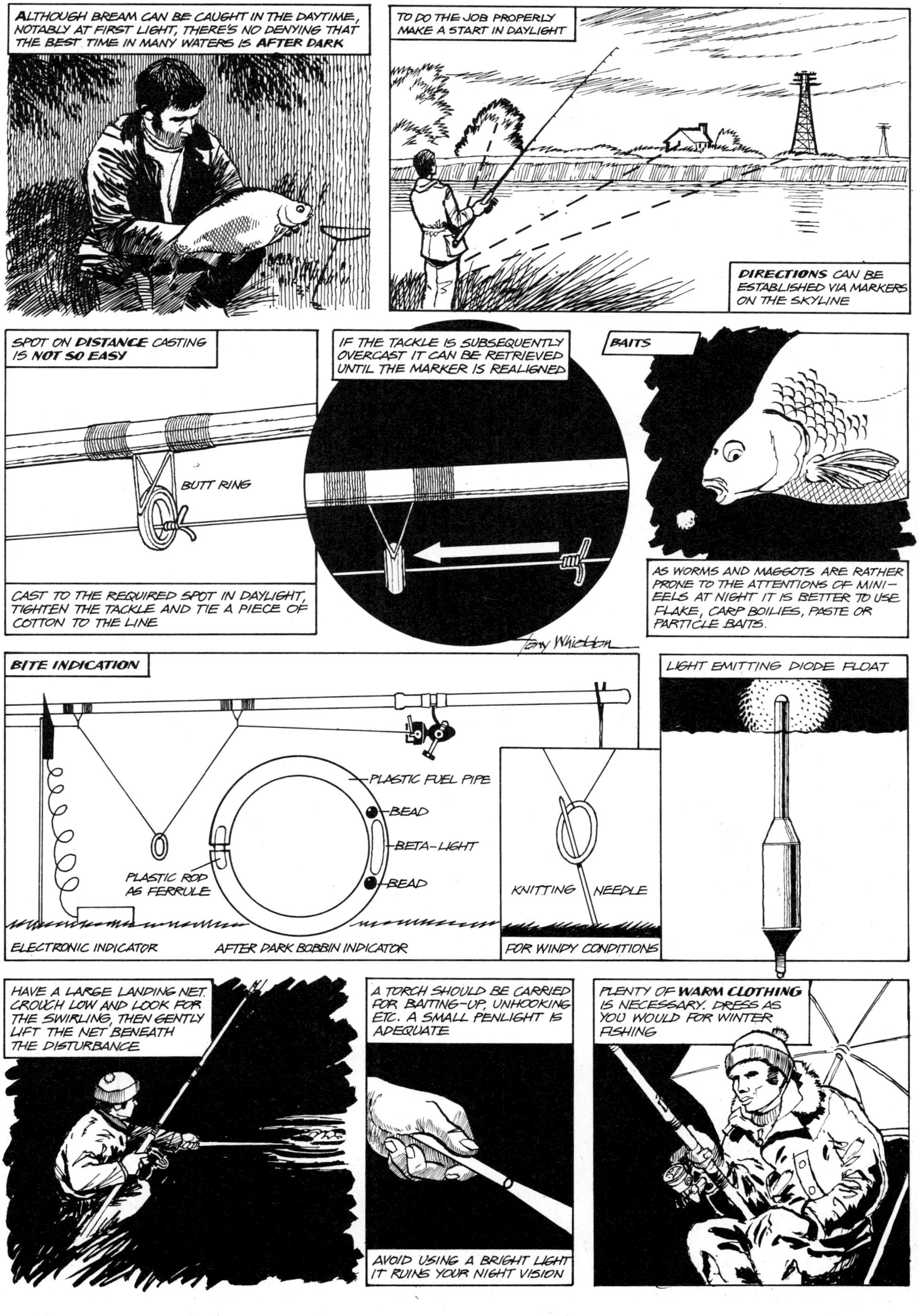

ALTHOUGH BREAM CAN BE CAUGHT IN THE DAYTIME, NOTABLY AT FIRST LIGHT, THERE'S NO DENYING THAT THE BEST TIME IN MANY WATERS IS AFTER DARK
TO DO THE JOB PROPERLY MAKE A START IN DAYLIGHT
DIRECTIONS CAN BE ESTABLISHED VIA MARKERS ON THE SKYLINE
SPOT ON DISTANCE CASTING IS NOT SO EASY
BUTT RING
CAST TO THE REQUIRED SPOT IN DAYLIGHT, TIGHTEN THE TACKLE AND TIE A PIECE OF COTTON TO THE LINE
IF THE TACKLE IS SUBSEQUENTLY OVERCAST IT CAN BE RETRIEVED UNTIL THE MARKER IS REALIGNED
BAITS
AS WORMS AND MAGGOTS ARE RATHER PRONE TO THE ATTENTIONS OF MINI-EELS AT NIGHT IT IS BETTER TO USE FLAKE, CARP BOILIES, PASTE OR PARTICLE BAITS.
Tony Whieldon
BITE INDICATION
PLASTIC FUEL PIPE
BEAD
BETA-LIGHT
BEAD
PLASTIC ROD AS FERRULE
ELECTRONIC INDICATOR
AFTER DARK BOBBIN INDICATOR
KNITTING NEEDLE
FOR WINDY CONDITIONS
LIGHT EMITTING DIODE FLOAT
HAVE A LARGE LANDING NET. CROUCH LOW AND LOOK FOR THE SWIRLING, THEN GENTLY LIFT THE NET BENEATH THE DISTURBANCE
A TORCH SHOULD BE CARRIED FOR BAITING-UP, UNHOOKING ETC. A SMALL PENLIGHT IS ADEQUATE
AVOID USING A BRIGHT LIGHT IT RUINS YOUR NIGHT VISION
PLENTY OF WARM CLOTHING IS NECESSARY. DRESS AS YOU WOULD FOR WINTER FISHING

STILLWATER FISHING

BIG BREAM CHALLENGE

THERE was a brief period a few years ago when big bream were devalued. Colossal fish into double figures were trapped from Abberton Reservoir, Essex and transferred to waters incapable of supporting them.

For a couple of seasons those bream were caught from all sorts of insignificant puddles and trickles in the south-east and to the casual observer they were indistinguishable from hard-earned specimens taken from waters where they had grown large naturally.

Now sanity has been restored. Only those fish placed in quality waters survived, the others rapidly lost weight and died.

A 10 lb. bream is an enormous fish and probably one of the most difficult "targets" in coarse fishing. Few anglers have every seen one, let alone caught one. My biggest was 8 lb. so if you are looking for advice as to how you may catch a double-figure fish I have to tell you that I'm not your man!

Anyone can catch bream to 5 lb. or so, but where do you look for the bigger-than-average specimens, the 6, 7 and 8 pounders? Reservoirs have a good track record, notably Abberton—although restrictions placed on where and when you may fish probably make it a poor choice—and Tring, Hertfordshire. Gravel-pits often hold big fish but they can be extraordinarily difficult to tempt—even the shoals of average size fish can seemingly disappear for weeks on end.

Although associated with deep water—almost every bream water having its obligatory "bream 'ole"—some of the biggest I've seen have been in quite shallow water. It is by no means unusal to see them rolling or bow-waving on shallow bars and plateaux early in the morning.

Look for them wherever there is a sudden depth change, such as a shelf. Really deep gullies are unproductive, but a gully only a few inches deeper than its surrounding area may well be part of a patrol route.

Lots of people have written about these patrol routes but I've never seen anyone refer to the fishes' territorial instincts. One pit where I occasionally fish has three main shoals and the fish in each are physically different in appearance and occupy different size-bands.

It's amazing how they keep to their own area of the pit. They feed best when a wind blows towards their chosen territory but unlike carp they don't follow the wind from one side of the pit to the other.

Bream are shoal fish and remain in the same group throughout their lives. That's why the biggest fish are found either individually or in two's and three's, the rest of the shoal having fallen foul of predators, disease, old-age or bad handling by anglers.

Big bream are genuinely tackle-shy. Lots of fish have this reputation but bream are among the few that really deserve it. I have no doubt at all that you'll get more bites on 2 lb. line than on 4 lb. line and as bream aren't exactly renowned for their fighting ability, light lines are quite viable, as are small hooks.

TACKLE SHY

My usual tackle choice is 3½ lb. main line, 2½ lb. hook-line and hook sizes 18 to 12 depending on bait. I'm not a fan of short legering rods such as those popular with matchmen; mine are thin-walled, fast-taper 11-footers.

Bream are tackle-shy but they are not shy biters. I've read all about shy-biting bream and how difficult they are to hook so I have to concede that some bream must behave that way, but mine don't. I get problems with deep-hooking and this worries me because they are fragile fish and don't take kindly to a disgorger being pushed down their throats.

I can't help wondering if some specimen-hunters make problems for themselves by using the sort of terminal tackle that would be unlikely to deceive a mentally defective "skimmer", let alone a 7 or 8 lb. bream. Short tails, coarse line, large hooks . . . no wonder tiny bites are sometimes all they get.

Then there is the problem of line-bites. Bream give lovely sailaway bites when they swim into a leger line and they do so frequently in a baited pitch. The answer is to fish fine and use a bobbin on a 2 ft. drop between first and second rings and wait for the bream to "hang" themselves. I usualy wait for the reel to turn before giving a token strike. I know it sounds primitive and crude but it works.

I've tried all sorts of terminal tackles for long-range legering and have come to favour the fixed paternoster. I know, in theory, that fish should feel the lead and drop the bait and that, in theory, a running lead should prove to be much more efficient. In practice, however, running leads are much less efficient than theorists claim.

I tie a blood-loop in my main line about 9 in. from the lead. To this loop is tied the hook-line which is usually about 4 ft. long and only in exceptional circumstances will it be much less such as times when by shortening the tail the problem of continual deep-hooking can sometimes be reduced. Or maybe I'll be fishing small pockets in weed where a long tail could be a liability.

Although I've referred to the use of a lead, I mostly use the largest size Drennan "Feeder-link" and to ensure that its contents are emptied immediately it hits bottom I use it upside-down and open-ended.

Traditionally, specimen hunters fish for bream over a carpet of bread stodge but I am convinced this is not the best approach. Far better to bait the area with half a dozen catapult deliveries of fine crumb laced with high quality feed like casters or squatts. Top-up feeding will occur naturally during the session with the "Feederlink".

The three most effective baits are maggots with gozzers as the best, breadflake and small redworms.

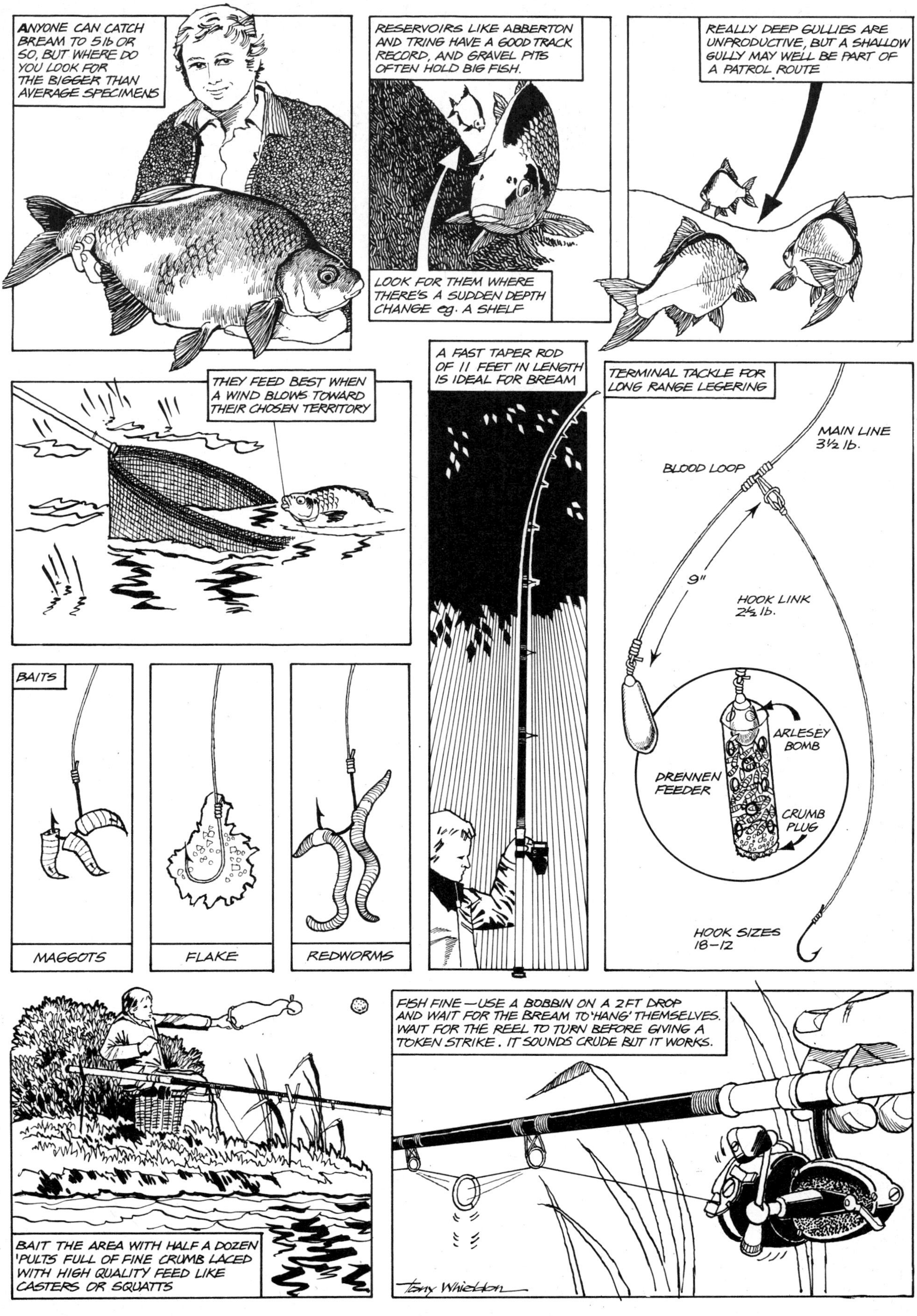
ANYONE CAN CATCH BREAM TO 5lb OR SO, BUT WHERE DO YOU LOOK FOR THE BIGGER THAN AVERAGE SPECIMENS
RESERVOIRS LIKE ABBERTON AND TRING HAVE A GOOD TRACK RECORD, AND GRAVEL PITS OFTEN HOLD BIG FISH.
LOOK FOR THEM WHERE THERE'S A SUDDEN DEPTH CHANGE eg. A SHELF
REALLY DEEP GULLIES ARE UNPRODUCTIVE, BUT A SHALLOW GULLY MAY WELL BE PART OF A PATROL ROUTE
THEY FEED BEST WHEN A WIND BLOWS TOWARD THEIR CHOSEN TERRITORY
A FAST TAPER ROD OF 11 FEET IN LENGTH IS IDEAL FOR BREAM
TERMINAL TACKLE FOR LONG RANGE LEGERING
MAIN LINE 3½ lb.
BLOOD LOOP
9"
HOOK LINK 2½ lb.
ARLESEY BOMB
DRENNEN FEEDER
CRUMB PLUG
HOOK SIZES 18–12
BAITS
MAGGOTS
FLAKE
REDWORMS
BAIT THE AREA WITH HALF A DOZEN 'PULTS FULL OF FINE CRUMB LACED WITH HIGH QUALITY FEED LIKE CASTERS OR SQUATTS
FISH FINE—USE A BOBBIN ON A 2FT DROP AND WAIT FOR THE BREAM TO 'HANG' THEMSELVES. WAIT FOR THE REEL TO TURN BEFORE GIVING A TOKEN STRIKE. IT SOUNDS CRUDE BUT IT WORKS.
Tony Whieldon

STILLWATER FISHING

IN SEARCH OF BIG ROACH

BIG roach may be found in rivers but there's no doubt in my mind that the largest are to be found in stillwaters, notably in reservoirs and gravel pits.

The track record of such waters supports this view. Fish to just over 4 lb have been recorded from Grafham and the traps at Abberton, Essex, have produced them almost as big. Prior to their dramatic decline the London reservoirs were the best-known big roach waters in the country, producing many big fish.

The current record of 4 lb 1 oz was a gravel-pit fish but pits are contrary places at the best of times and few anglers are willing to invest the required amount of time and effort even though the potential rewards are considerable.

That is really the crux of the matter—the search for big roach in large sheets of stillwater can be a soul-destroying activity. True, there are lakes and pits where big roach can be taken easily but such places are rare.

The biggest problem is undoubtedly location for with few exceptions roach tend to be scare in waters where they grow really big. When faced with 50 or more acres of windswept pit, or several hundred acres of reservoir, where do you start?

First, obtain an accurate picture of the bottom contours with a plummet or, better still, an echo-sounder. Many species of fish are attracted to shelves and drop-offs and roach are no exception. They are also partial to medium-depth plateaux, particularly if the area is a long way out and flanked by deeper water on at least one side.

My definition of medium depth is about ten feet. Twenty feet plus is deep and less than 3 ft is shallow.

If the chosen water is a reservoir I recommend looking for places on the bank where sand or shingle have been built up by wave action. There will almost certainly be such an area somewhere on the north bank, probably in the north-east corner, which receives the prevailing south westerlies. There will very likely by a similar spot somewhere on the south bank due to winter northerlies.

Why should such places be attractive to roach? It is tempting to assume it has something to do with food being washed there by current and wind, but I have doubts about that theory. It could, however, be due to adjacent silt deposits and their consequent fertility.

Pebbles, shingle and coarse sand are heavy and are therefore deposited as soon as the waves lose their impetus after breaking on the shoreline. Silt is much lighter and continues to be carried in suspension until sub-surface currents have slacked almost to a standstill.

The distance from the windward bank at which this happens depends on depth, bank configuration and, of course, the strength of the wind. It may be as close as 20 yards to the bank in deep water, or four or five times that distance if it is shallow. Generally, I would expect these fertile silt deposits to be from 30 to 60 yards out.

In a reservoir or gravel pit I always choose to fish into the wind as this is a key factor on big exposed waters. The only time I would choose not to fish directly facing the wind is when wave action has made the water thick and dirty with suspended sand. I suspect that most fish avoid sandy water to protect their delicate gill filaments from irritation.

Roach sometimes prime on the surface and as this activity often accompanies, or immediately precedes feeding, it should never be ignored. It doesn't matter if the priming is being done over 20 ft or more of water—sooner or later they'll get their heads down and feed. I know it seems illogical for fish to roll on the surface when their feeding area lies 20 ft below them, but it happens.

Close-in fishing with float tackle will take big roach. William Penney caught his one-time record from Lambeth Reservoir in this manner but legering is usually the best bet and my choice would be long-range feeder-fishing.

The largest size Drennan feeder, when fully loaded with squatts held in place by a plug of damp crumb and weighted with just one or two swan shot, weighs in the region of 1½ to 2 oz (42 gm to 56 gm). That dictates a main line of no less then 3½ lb test or snap-offs will occur while casting.

If the range is such that additional lead is needed then the line strength will have to be upped accordingly, but there is never any need to go heavier than 5 lb test.

This maxi-range work is done with a lead of up to 1 oz embedded in the top of the feeder. Some anglers use Araldite to fix the lead in position but I've not found it necessary.

The hook-line should be as fine as practical. I would regard 2½ lb test as maximum and most times opt for something between 1½ lb and 2 lb.

Hooks should always be as small as possible. Big roach will take big baits on large hooks and coarse lines—I once had a 2 lb plus fish while eel fishing and it swallowed a size 2 hook on 15 lb cable-laid wire trace—But only a fool sets out to catch roach on heavy gear.

You'll get far more takes on fine tackle. I don't think roach are clever, or even crafty as is sometimes claimed, but I do think they have a well-developed sense of caution.

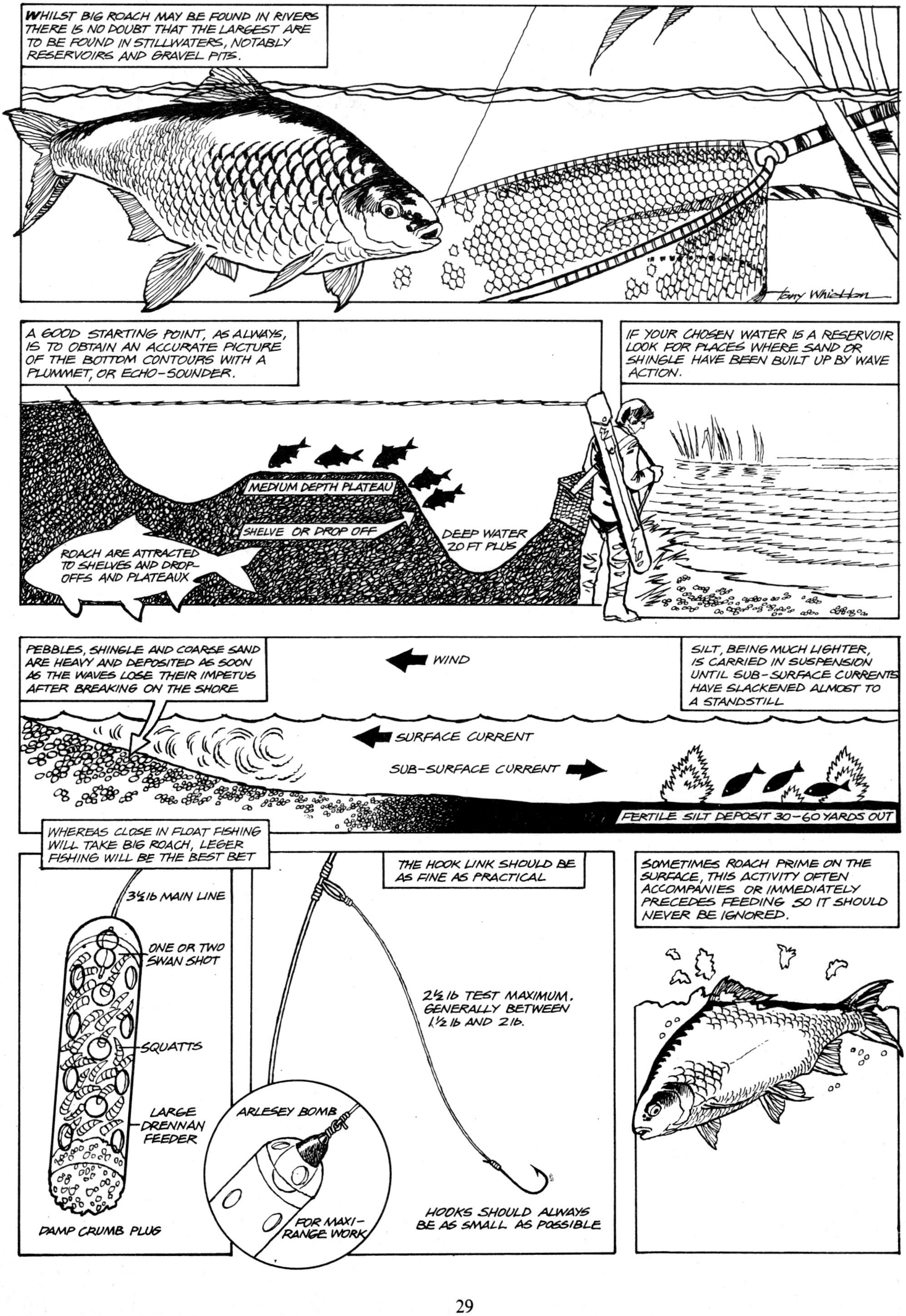
WHILST BIG ROACH MAY BE FOUND IN RIVERS THERE IS NO DOUBT THAT THE LARGEST ARE TO BE FOUND IN STILLWATERS, NOTABLY RESERVOIRS AND GRAVEL PITS.
Tony Whieldon
A GOOD STARTING POINT, AS ALWAYS, IS TO OBTAIN AN ACCURATE PICTURE OF THE BOTTOM CONTOURS WITH A PLUMMET, OR ECHO-SOUNDER.
MEDIUM DEPTH PLATEAU
SHELVE OR DROP OFF
DEEP WATER 20 FT PLUS
ROACH ARE ATTRACTED TO SHELVES AND DROP-OFFS AND PLATEAUX
IF YOUR CHOSEN WATER IS A RESERVOIR LOOK FOR PLACES WHERE SAND OR SHINGLE HAVE BEEN BUILT UP BY WAVE ACTION.
PEBBLES, SHINGLE AND COARSE SAND ARE HEAVY AND DEPOSITED AS SOON AS THE WAVES LOSE THEIR IMPETUS AFTER BREAKING ON THE SHORE
WIND
SILT, BEING MUCH LIGHTER, IS CARRIED IN SUSPENSION UNTIL SUB-SURFACE CURRENTS HAVE SLACKENED ALMOST TO A STANDSTILL
SURFACE CURRENT
SUB-SURFACE CURRENT
FERTILE SILT DEPOSIT 30-60 YARDS OUT
WHEREAS CLOSE IN FLOAT FISHING WILL TAKE BIG ROACH, LEGER FISHING WILL BE THE BEST BET
3½ lb MAIN LINE
ONE OR TWO SWAN SHOT
SQUATTS
LARGE DRENNAN FEEDER
DAMP CRUMB PLUG
ARLESEY BOMB
FOR MAXI-RANGE WORK
THE HOOK LINK SHOULD BE AS FINE AS PRACTICAL
2½ lb TEST MAXIMUM. GENERALLY BETWEEN 1½ lb AND 2 lb.
HOOKS SHOULD ALWAYS BE AS SMALL AS POSSIBLE
SOMETIMES ROACH PRIME ON THE SURFACE, THIS ACTIVITY OFTEN ACCOMPANIES OR IMMEDIATELY PRECEDES FEEDING SO IT SHOULD NEVER BE IGNORED.

STILLWATER FISHING TOP THREE ROACH BAITS

IF I had to pin my faith on just three baits for big roach I would choose, in order of preference, bread, maggots and worms.

When bread is mentioned most anglers think of flake but my choice would be compressed crust. Very few anglers use this bait these days, yet it's one of the most effective bread baits of all. To get the best from the bait it needs to be prepared at home, ideally 24 hours before use.

RIGHT LOAF

The first requirement is the right sort of loaf with a very close-grained crust. A square-tin white sandwich loaf is ideal. This can be used fresh for about 48 hours but I keep mine in the refrigerator. This two-day delay is not essential but helps to guarantee results.

Cut off the crusts and place the crumb side down on a damp tea-towel. If the tea-towel is wetted and then wrung out very tightly it will be about right. A second damp tea-towel is placed on top of the crust and a board placed on top of that.

A heavy weight is then put on top of the lot. Two or three mail order catalogues are about right! Leave for about 12 hours then carefully remove the compressed crust from between the tea-towels.

The crust may be taken to the waterside in slabs and cut to hook-bait size as required or diced to size at home. I prefer to dice it at home and keep it in an airtight container or it will dry out and lose its special qualities.

Crust prepared in this way sinks—but only just. That's important as it then sits nicely on top of soft mud or silkweed. Not that its use is confined to soft bottoms, the fact that it is easily sucked up and swirled about is, I'm sure, part of the appeal.

Another advantage of pressed crust is that it is much tougher than unprepared crust. The damp press process gives it a sort of rubbery consistency which withstands long-casting but in no way impedes the hook on the strike.

Bites are usually very confident. The indicator goes all the way without hesitation and often without any preamble.

I usually cut my crust cubes in two sizes of $1/4$ inch and $3/8$ inch, used with fine-wire medium-shank eyed hooks, sizes 14 and 12 respectively. My favourite hook for this sort of fishing—and for most other sorts of fishing, is a Sealey 1714B.

When baiting up, the hook is passed carefully right through the crust so that it emerges on the crumb side. It is then turned through 180 degrees and gently pulled back into the crust.

MATCH BOOM

The boom in match fishing in recent years has resulted in top quality maggots becoming widely available and most tackle shops now offer a range of colours as well as squatts and pinkies.

Different colours possibly have a place in specimen hunting, but I'm happy enough with ordinary natural whites. But I insist they are fresh and clean.

For single maggot I use a size 18 fine wire spade-end hook; for double or treble maggot I increase size to a 16.

Worms are perhaps more relevant to rivers but they have their day on stillwaters from time to time. I haven't taken many stillwater roach on worm while using it as a roach bait for the simple reason that my conversion to it in this context has been quite recent.

I knew that stillwater roach took worms quite readily, of course, but I didn't really consider it as a serious contender. What forced me to re-think my attitude was the number of good roach I took on worm while fishing for other species. One afternoon in summer I took well over half-a-hundredweight of roach on worm in about three hours. That catch, and others, included fish in the 2 lb class.

The worms which proved so effective were "reds"—not those obscure, anonymous reddish-coloured worms dug from a muck-heap. Brandlings were less effective and mini-lobs still less effective.

Large worms—a large redworm is only about three inches long—are fished on a size 12 (Sealey 1724B again) hooked just once through the head. Smaller worms and half-worms are fished on a size 14.

For feed I rely on squatts or casters plus a small quantity of hempseed. I fully subscribe to the view that hemp has a special ability to attract and hold roach but it is very filling and must be used sparingly. I would not expect to use more than a quarter-of-a pint for a day's fishing.

For most long-range roach fishing, the tackle set-up is a standard paternoster feeder-rig with the three to four feet long hook-link tied to a bloodloop about nine inches above the feeder.

This series was first published in ANGLER'S MAIL during the summer of 1981 and has been specially adapted for this edition of Angler's Mail Annual.

TOP THREE FOR BIG ROACH
Tony Whieldon
TO PREPARE COMPRESSED CRUST CUT THE CRUSTS FROM A SQUARE-TIN SANDWICH LOAF AND PLACE CRUMB SIDE DOWN ON A DAMP TEA TOWEL
PLACE ANOTHER DAMP TEA TOWEL ON TOP OF THE CRUSTS THEN COVER WITH A BOARD. ON TOP OF THE WHOLE LOT PLACE A HEAVY WEIGHT.
MAIL ORDER
SUMMER 1981
LEAVE FOR ABOUT 12 HOURS THEN CAREFULLY REMOVE THE COMPRESSED CRUST FROM BETWEEN THE TOWELS
THE CRUST MAY EITHER BE TAKEN TO THE WATERSIDE IN SLABS AND CUT AS REQUIRED OR IT CAN BE DICED TO SIZE AT HOME
ADVANTAGES OF COMPRESSED CRUST
SITS NICELY ON SOFT MUD OR SILKWEED
WITHSTANDS LONG CASTING
PRODUCES CONFIDENT BITES
BAITING UP WITH CRUST CUBES
SIZE 14 OR 12 SEALEY 1714B MEDIUM SHANK EYED HOOK
BAITING UP WITH MAGGOTS
SIZE 18 FINE WIRE SPADE END HOOK
SIZE 16
3" REDWORM
SIZE 12 SEALEY 1714 B
SIZE 14 SEALEY 1714 B
SMALLER REDWORM

SUCCESS STORY

How I caught my 38¼ pounder!

Kevin Maddocks with the 35-pounder he caught shortly after his Ashlea Pool success.

AFTER four seasons of trailing an upper-30 lb carp I had seen many times around Ashlea Pool, in Gloucestershire, I was beginning to think I would never catch it.

My plans to intercept this particular fish were well-laid but for some reason it had never ventured near any of my baits until I returned for a session of three days and two nights, little knowing I was at last to catch my dream fish . . . but only after some hair-raising experiences.

Over the seasons at Ashlea, which is controlled by Peter Mohan, I had landed one carp over 30 lb, plus seven "twenties", mainly by spotting where they were feeding. On arrival this time I walked round the pool looking for the carp, but a breeze blew into the deeper end of the pool, about seven feet deep, with surface ripples that made it impossible to spot fish properly.

I climbed a tree overlooking the place where I thought they might be and saw several large specimens, including a couple of "thirties". But I wasn't interested as I had eyes only for the biggest fish in the pool, which was cruising around the group.

I crouched in the tree, watching every move as they swam in a clear patch among a mass of dark weeds. Every so often they sank slowly out of sight on the lower lily weeds. Bubbles broke surface all round them and I knew they were feeding.

I put out some floating baits in the swim upwind of the carp but they showed no interest. So by about noon of the first day I set up my tackle in the swim nearest to where I had seen the fish feeding and planned to fish with two rods—one into the clear hole and the other right in the thickest part of the dense patch of "cabbages".

The bait put into the clear hole was my own special concoction consisting of a high protein mix, mainly milk food with an egg binder, flavoured with butter. Each bait was rolled into quarter-inch balls and cast out about 15 yards.

My other bait was similar but I had to fish it in a special way by somehow blasting through the cabbages with a big lead so that the bait was in clear water under the layer of cabbages.

A lot of thought went into this problem and I finally came up with what I thought was a winner (*see diagram*). I chose a 2 oz. Arlesey bomb to smash through the weed but still had the problem of keeping the tail, bait and hook from tangling up.

KEVIN'S PVA RIG

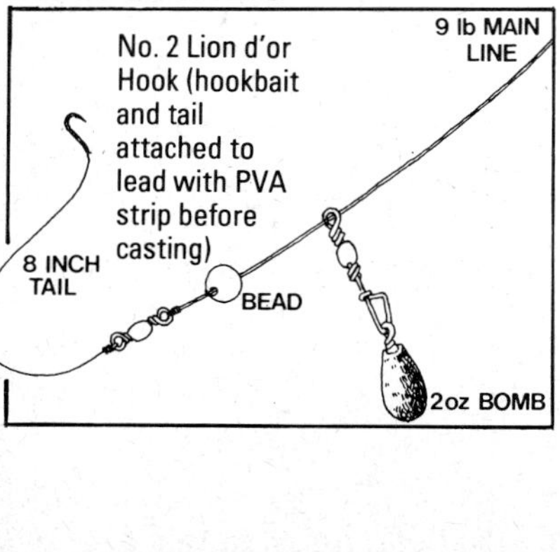

In the end I kept the tail to a minimum, about eight inches long, and used a strip of PVA to fix the baited hook near the lead. When I cast out, the lead broke through the layer of cabbages and the bait was left lying free on the bottom of the pool.

Once the rods were set up I baited the area heavily and sat back and waited. Around 2 p.m. that afternoon I had a line bite but the fish "spooked" and moved out of the swim. From then, right round until the following afternoon, nothing happened. As night fell I settled in for another wait full of expectations, but there was no action.

TREE-TOP SPOTTING

On the following day I carried on stalking, still hoping I was going to catch, and this proved to be the first day in four years when I was to have a definite chance at the fish I was after.

I spotted the carp while I was up a tree and decided to try and hook it. When I climbed down I lost sight of the fish because of the "chop" and glare on the surface of the pool but I was so determined to catch the fish, come what may, that I took my rod back up the tree with me and flicked out a free offering of breadflake.

To my amazement the carp took it! By now I was pretty excited and cast out a second piece of flake and this time it had a hook embedded in it. As it sank the fish followed it down, looked at it for a while, circled, touched it with its lips and then decided not to have it.

I don't really know what I would have done if I had actually hooked the fish. On reflection, I would have probably jumped out of the tree, even though it was fifteen feet off the ground. I was prepared to go to any lengths to land the fish!

By evening all the fish had returned to my swims and were feeding like mad and I settled down for the second night confident that something was going to happen. I rebaited the swim and even set up a third rod and cast to where the bubbles were rising.

After dark it rained heavily and I immediately lost confidence. When the rain finally stopped the wind dropped and it went very cold. All the signs started to look right and I knew I was going to get some action.

Around 2 a.m. I had a six-inch lift bite on my left hand rod but this didn't develop into anything. An hour later I had a couple of four-inch twitches on my new rod which had a PVA taped bait. This didn't develop into anything immediately, but 30 minutes later I had what I call a "jerky" take.

I struck immediately and met solid resistance. It was pitch dark and I had no idea what was happening as I couldn't feel any movement and thought I had been weeded.

I kept up as much pressure as I dared and then it dawned on me—I wasn't weeded, the carp was slowly moving off to my left. At this point I noticed the bobbin on my left-hand rod rise and thought I was into a second fish but, of course, fish No. 1 had kited right in front of me and picked up one of my other lines.

The carp headed for the cover of the overhanging trees and I lowered my rod and pumped like mad to counter the action. Once in front of me the fish was ready for the net . . . beaten in a couple of minutes after four years of hunting for it. Then disaster struck!

I dropped my other two rods off their rests and picked up the landing net but as I pushed the net out into the dark everything fouled up, with the mesh of the net tangled around my two spare rods.

Taking a big gamble I pushed aside the two spare rods and fouled-up landing net, released the bale arm of the reel, put the rod back in the rests and dashed up the bank for a second smaller net, which I use for stalking.

The net was not really big enough as the gap was only 30 inches wide but in the circumstances it was the only thing I could do. Luckily, when I returned the fish was still on and I was thankful not to be using barbless hooks.

My net was so small I had to peer through the dark and wait until I saw the nose of the fish touch the spreader block of the net. When I was sure the fish was in the net I hauled it out.

As I saw it on the grass I felt jubilant. At first I thought it went 40 lb—the Ashlea fish everyone wanted to catch—but it scaled 38 lb 4 oz to establish a new record for the water and a personal best for me.

In a sequel to this amazing story, I visited a Kent day-ticket water 15 days after catching this fish and had the good fortune to land another carp weighing 35 lbs.

•*First published in Angler's Mail, October 15, 1980.*

LOG

Date: 17th September 1980.
Venue: Ashlea Pool, Gloucestershire.
Catch: 38¼ lb. carp.
Captor: Kevin Maddocks of Enfield, Middlesex.

What it's all about! The right bait in the right place at the right time and an angler with sufficient experience to convert a chance into success as a Fenland pike hunter takes on a fighting specimen.

PICTURE: BARRIE RICKARDS

TOP MARKS!

Ivan Marks, a partner in the thriving Leicester tackle firm of Marks and Marlow, is an internationally-famous match angler and has built up a unique following of admirers throughout the sport. His weekly column in Angler's Mail is a favourite with thousands of regular readers. Here, in picture form, Ivan demonstrates his skill at legering for bream, the species which helped to make his name.

Left: Correct use of a bait catapult is essential if a steady supply of groundbait is to land in the right place. Ivan keeps his arm straight and shows how it's done.

Left: Ivan watches the tip of his leger rod ready for instant action. Note how the rod is positioned on a wide-neck rod-rest with the rest of his gear placed carefully around him, everything at hand.

Above: A bream has taken the bait and Ivan responds immediately by lifting the rod high and striking firmly and cleanly.

Right: Bream and Ivan Marks go together like bread and cheese. Most of his big catches of bream have come on leger tackle and this picture shows what a few hours in a good swim can achieve.

PICTURES: ANGLER'S MAIL LIBRARY

Carp breeding is a highly skilled business. Few have attempted it on a commercial scale in Britain but the Symons family have overcome all the difficulties to become one of the most successful. Working in conjunction with the Lea Division of Thames Water Authority, they have reared thousands of carp at their Fisher's Green Farm in Hertfordshire, providing new stocks for a variety of fisheries in the Thames area and for private waters in Norfolk. Martin Symons is pictured with a small consignment bound for a one-way journey to Waveney Valley Lakes at Wortwell, Norfolk.

PICTURE: ANGLER'S MAIL LIBRARY

Right: Hairy moments as an ill-tempered conger eel is gaffed aboard a West Country wreck-fishing boat.

Below (right): Alf Green, of Sussex, using a butt pad to steady his powerful rod as he copes with a lively conger hooked on a trip in the Rye boat, "Norvic".

Below (left): The spoils of a long day at sea. John Head, from Sherborne, Dorset, displays a superb 42 1b. ling captured at a wreck mark from the Plymouth boat, "Zummerzet Maid".

PICTURES: MIKE MILLMAN AND ANGLER'S MAIL LIBRARY

Wreck fishing in deep water is no game for the weak or faint-hearted. Heavy fish hooked at great depths do not give up easily and demand firm muscles, a strong back and lots of spirit before the catch is safely aboard.

HOW'S YOUR LUCK?

Some anglers christen their first rod with a specimen fish. That's fisherman's luck. Some try an extra last cast before packing up and strike it rich. That's gambler's luck. But for those who slog away, season after season, with growing skill and a determination to succeed, it's not luck—just fair doings! These two pages of specimens are dedicated to them.

Right: These handsome tench topped a memorable day at an Oxfordshire gravel pit. Both fish tipped the scales at 7¾ 1b.

Far right: The wily club can defeat the best but this fine 4 lb. 14 oz. specimen from Oxfordshire's River Windrush came to the bank just long enough to pose for an angler who knew an extra trick or two.

Above: Carp fishing is virtually a sport in itself with a happy band of devoted followers who think of precious little else. This double-figure specimen is a bench mark, to be followed by 30-pounders—plus for the most successful.

Right: Barbel fishing is another specialist sport that is not always available due to the uneven distribution of the species. But they are one of the most eagerly sought fighting fish and, pound for pound, give more action thrills than most.

Left: Perch stocks have recovered after a mystery disease that wiped out stocks in most places. Few fish are so handsome or boldly marked. This beauty fell for a spinner, a delicate art for those who travel light and quietly.

Right: Plugs and spinners are sometimes as irresistible to anglers as they are to pike! But in the right hands a bright lure is a deadly and fascinating form of pike fishing and will account for many specimens like this.

Dry Fly Magic

DRY FLY MAGIC

by TED ANDREWS

THERE is a special fascination about the traditional dry flies, a fascination that for me never tires. Perhaps it is because they are at the very heart of fly tying and illustrate that a pinch of fur, a feather from a cockerel's neck and a twist of wire can be conjured together to create an almost living creature.

The flies illustrated here include nine of the best-known patterns which have been tried and tested over the years and can be guaranteed to bring pleasure in the tying results on the river bank.

1. LUNN'S PARTICULAR

Hook: 16-14 UE
Silk: Crimson
Tail: Four fibres from a natural red cock hackle
Wings: Two medium-blue dun hackle tips
Hackle: Natural red cock hackle

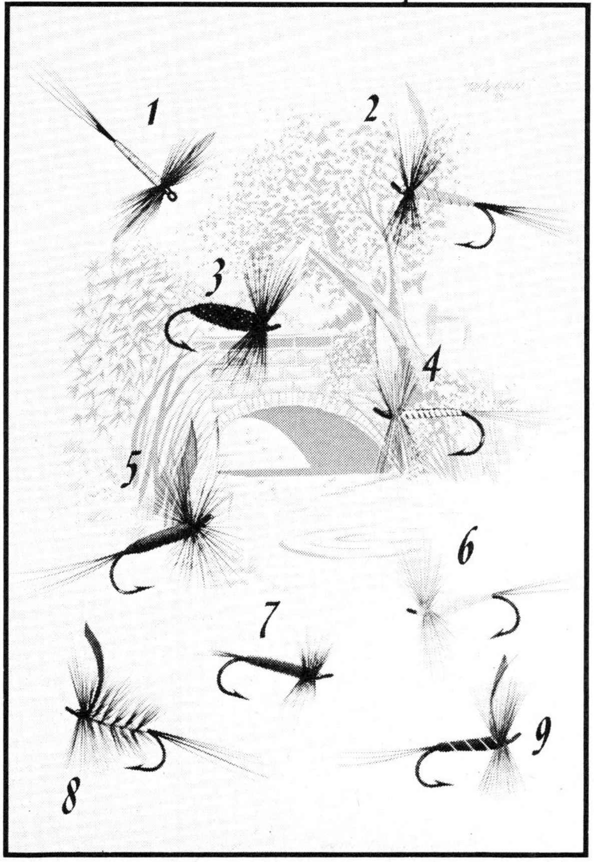

KEY

1 Lunn's Particular
2 Greenwell's Glory
3 Coachman
4 Ginger Quill
5 Iron Blue Dun
6 Tup's Indispensable
7 Grey Duster
8 Wickham's Fancy
9 Rough Olive

2. GREENWELL'S GLORY

Hook: 12-14 UE
Silk: Yellow
Tail: A few fibres of furnace (alternatively ginger) cock hackle fibres
Body: Formed from the tying silk which should be thoroughly waxed to impart an olive hue to the body
Rib: Fine gold wire
Wings: Slips of blackbird wing feather
Hackle: Coch-y-bondhu or furnace

3. COACHMAN

Hook: 12-16 UE
Silk: Black
Body: Bronze peacock herl
Wings: White duck wing quill
Hackle: Natural red

4. GINGER QUILL

Hook: 14-16 UE
Silk: Black
Tail: Fibres from a ginger cock hackle
Body: A quill from the "eye" section of a peacock tail feather stripped of its herl
Wings: Starling wing quill
Hackle: Ginger cock

5. IRON BLUE DUN

Hook: 14-16 UE
Silk: Crimson
Tail: Fibres of blue dun cock hackle
Body: Dubbed mole's fur (remember to leave two or three turns of crimson tying silk exposed at the hook bend)
Wings: Darkest starling wing quill
Hackle: Darkest olive brown cock (dyed)

6. TUP'S INDISPENSABLE

Hook: 14-16 UE
Silk: Yellow
Tail: Blue dun cock hackle fibres
Body: Leave two or three exposed turns of yellow silk at the tail. The silk is then dubbed with pink seal's fur and wound up to the shoulder. Avoid a bright pink! By blending a mixture of white, yellow and red seal's fur a nice soft shade should be achieved.
Hackle: Blue dun
Another variation of the "Tups" gives a hackle of honey with tail whisks of a matching shade.

7. GREY DUSTER

Hook: 12-14 UE
Silk: Brown
Tail: Fibres of natural badger cock hackle
Body: Dubbed rabbit fur of a blue grey shade
Hackle: Stiff natural badger

8. WICKHAM'S FANCY

Hook: 14-16 UE
Silk: Black
Tail: Fibres of natural red game cock hackle
Body: Flat gold tinsel ribbed with gold wire
Body Hackle: Red game
Throat Hackle: Red game
Wings: Starling wing quill

9. ROUGH OLIVE

Hook: 14-16 UE
Silk: Olive
Tail: Dark olive cock hackle fibres
Rib: Fine gold wire
Body: Heron herl dyed olive
Wings: Starling wing quill
Hackle: Olive cock

ALAN PEARSON takes a close look at the traditional dry flies illustrated by Ted Andrews on page 40 and delves into the history of each fly, explaining what each fly is tied to imitate.

DRY FLY

WHEN studying a collection of traditional dry flies, the first thing to remember is that once a fly has become a household name over the years, it is because it is a very successful pattern. Fancy names given to many patterns do not help us at all in trying to establish just what it is that each dressing is supposed to imitate, That is why it can be difficult for a beginner to work out how best to fish each or every pattern for the best chance of success.

Clues can sometimes be found by looking back into the past to see how and where a pattern may have originated, and why. Then we have to try to separate fact from legend, which can cause more problems.

It is also true that many wet fly and nymph variations have been developed from the original dry fly tyings and methods of fishing.

Most, if not all, were created as river and stream patterns and although some have now transferred successfully to stillwater usage, their basic applications relate to moving water.

COACHMAN

The origins of this fly really are very obscure but the most common legend is that it was the original concept of a coachman to our Royal Family, possibly some time large last century. Indeed, there is a variation known as the Royal Coachman which might lend credence to the legend but which I suspect does nothing of the sort.

It is now less popular in this country but, surprisingly, is one of the most popular dry flies on the North American continent.

Probably devised as a river fly, it is now used mainly, and with killing effect, on the larger stillwaters, where it takes both brown and rainbow trout.

There are various theories about what the dressing is supposed to imitate but I am unable to accept any of these and prefer to regard it as a general-purpose deceiver. I have used it very successfully when trout have been rising freely to a hatch of sedges, or to the chironomid, or even to terrestial insects which have found their way on to the water in sufficient numbers to arouse the interest of the trout.

So if trout are rising to a fly of which you do not possess an imitation, put up a Coachman of appropriate size and you may well catch trout.

LUNN'S PARTICULAR

The origins of this fly are very well documented. William J. Lunn became a riverkeeper on the Test in about 1886 (a post subsequently occupied by his son Alfred and grandson Mick, who still remains in charge today). Strangely, the first Lunn did not appear to have taken any interest in fly tying until about 1916, and one of the first patterns he ever produced is probably the best-known of all his inventions.

Lunn's Particular is an extraordinarily successful imitation of the Medium Olive Spinner, particularly for chalk stream angling, but such seems to be its charm that it is reputedly the best general purpose chalkstream dry fly when trout are taking the spinner.

It is difficult to prove but this dressing has been claimed to be unusually successful in taking trout which become "spooky" when offered alternative patterns. So when any of the Olive family are up, particularly the Medium Olive, and trout are taking the spinner, the angler's first choice should be this great old pattern of Lunn's.

HISTORY

Scotland's River Tweed, home of Greenwell's Glory.

GREENWELL'S GLORY

This is another well-documented dressing. It appears that one day in May 1854, Canon William Greenwell, of Durham, was fishing the Sprouston Club water on the Tweed when a massive hatch of March Browns occurred but the brown trout ignored them, preferring to take another insect, of which the worthy Canon caught a sample or two.

These he presented the same evening to James Wright, the local professional fly dresser, who promptly tied some imitations which proved immediately successful, as they have been ever since.

One or two facts do not seem to quite fit the legend, however, because although Greenwell's Glory is undoubtedly an imitation of one of the Olive family, it is not exactly like any of them. Indeed, it appears more like a variant of an earlier imitation of the Dark Olive, although it has been suggested that it could have been a spurwing imitation.

I prefer to fish it when the trout are taking the Dark Olive dun, but there is no doubt it is a successful deceiver of brown trout when they are taking any of the olive duns.

IRON BLUE DUN

So many versions of this fly have been produced over so many years it is probably impossible to discover who should have the credit for devising it.

Basically, the Iron Blue is a small fly which appears very early in the season, particularly on cold days. Brown trout seem to find it almost irresistible, often picking it out of much larger hatches of other flies.

One or two of the chalk stream "ancients" believed it so attractive they used it throughout the season as their sole pattern. Their results seem to justify their faith but it could be said that much depends upon how you present an artificial to a trout. I would prefer to keep this fly in reserve, bringing it out only on those Spring days which have a decided nip in the air and when a hatch of Iron Blues can be seen to be occurring.

TUP'S INDISPENSABLE

R. S. Austin was a professional fly dresser in Tiverton. In 1900 he sent to the legendary G. E. M. Skues a sample of a new dressing he had developed and which had taken a number of large brown trout from the tributaries of the River Exe.

The dressing was stated to include hair taken from the scrotum of a ram (or tup) and in due course Skues christened the new pattern with the name by which we know it today.

Skues killed a great many fish with this new fly, passed on the information to others and it became one of the most successful and popular patterns of all time.

What Austin tied it to represent is quite a different matter. In many ways it appears to be a variation of his own Red Spinner pattern, which is tied to imitate the spinner of the Large Dark Olive, and yet there are inexplicable variations which call the matter into question. Neither does it conform well enough to any of the other Olive spinners to suggest that they had been used as a model.

Skues himself used to say that the Tup's Indispensable was useful as soon as the Pale Wateries appeared, usually during April, and some authorities hold it is a Pale Watery male spinner imitation; others suggest similarities with the Small Spurwing female spinner.

To my mind, Austin concocted by design or accident a very fine general-purpose imitation which serves well whether it is one or other of the Olives, or the Pale Watery, or even the Small Spurwing that is the fly on the water.

WICKHAM'S FANCY

Yet another trusty pattern, with obscure origins in the sense that this can only be described as probably not designed to imitate any particular member of any insect family, but which does well enough for an angler when almost anything is hatching, provided only that an effort is made to match the size of the artificial to the size of the hatching natural.

It will do very well when almost any variety of sedge is attracting the attention of trout, whether in river or

Tiverton fly dresser R. S. Austin tied the first Tups Indispensable, which he fished with some success on the River Exe in Devon.

stillwater, and will attract enough river brown trout when used in hatches of almost anything, except perhaps Mayfly and Iron Blue.

It does well enough for sea trout in rivers, rather than lochs, and in small sizes can prove immensely attractive to grayling. I am told it can be deadly for chub if a big well-hackled pattern is offered.

Some anglers swear by the winged version; others omit the wings and claim the hackle-only pattern is infinitely preferable. I have no strong feelings either way.

GREY DUSTER

Many anglers claim this to be the best of the all-round dry flies and there is much to recommend their viewpoint. It is not clear whether this was first devised as a river pattern but there is no doubt it seems to work equally well on stillwaters and streams.

Basically, we are back to a general-purpose dressing because the Grey Duster, tied large, has proved very successful for brown trout on lakes and rivers in Mayfly time; in a range of smaller sizes it can be a great killer when the Olives are up.

I have used it with considerable success for reservoir rainbows during sedge hatches and in very tiny versions during caenis hatches on small streams. It has stood in for the White Ghost Moth with remarkable results and fished static in clear water lakes when no fly has been on the water, it has succeeded in luring both brown and rainbow trout to their doom.

This is one of those fly patterns you need to own in a wide range of hook sizes—or not at all. There are no half-measures with the Grey Duster.

ROUGH OLIVE

At one time it could have been said there were as many different versions of the Rough Olive as there were anglers tying their own dry flies. Even today I doubt it is possible to define a "correct" pattern.

Strictly speaking, it may have originated as an imitation of the Early Olive dun but opinions can differ as to what exactly is meant by Early Olive.

So for the sake of harmony, let us assume a dual function for the beast; it can imitate both the Iron Blue dun and the Dark Olive dun. Indeed, by including all known variations in size and colour it may fairly be said it can be used to represent each and every one of the duns of the whole wide family of Olives.

GINGER QUILL

For some reason, quill-bodied dry flies became very popular on chalk-streams, although their hard, clear outline ought to have appeared to the trout as far less lifelike and "insecty" than herl bodies.

Basically the quill body is obtained by stripping the herl from a feather and winding the denuded quill tightly round the hook to produce a segmented or banded body. Different effects were created by the use of different coloured wings, hackles and tails; thus—"Red Quill", "Blue Quill" and so on.

The use of larger or smaller hooks, variation in colour and differing wing positions meant that by using the simple basic quill body, dressing variations could imitate a vast range of natural insects. But it has not been at all uncommon for anglers to worry more about accurate sizing than colour match and so this is yet another general-purpose pattern.

CONCLUSION. After this brief study of nine of the most justifiably popular and rewarding dry flies, an interesting fact emerges. In just one case, the Iron Blue, we have a dressing which sets out to imitate just one specific insect and which succeeds admirably. In every other case, usage varies from very wide general-purpose to more selective usage, but still covering a number of possibilities.

This rather gives the lie to those who have suggested through the years that dry fly fishing is the pinnacle of the fly fishing art; that every fly has to be a completely perfect imitation of just one natural insect form.

No doubt there are such flies, and anglers who use them, but the facts detailed here suggest that the most lastingly popular flies of all are those which can be used in all manner of ways to deceive trout which are feeding selectively on just one sort of fly.

In my humble opinion, this means that the cleverest flies of all are those which can be all things to all trout. Therefore, those worthy gentlemen who devised the patterns must be the cleverest tyers of dry flies.

KING OF THE TENCH!

Melvyn Russ tells the story behind the capture of Britain's biggest tench, 10 lb 1¼ oz.

I HAVE seen a number of record fish during my years with *Angler's Mail,* including the biggest roach and conger. But the fish I really wanted to be on the spot for was a record tench.

My chance came on the second morning of the 1981 coarse season when *Angler's Mail* News Desk took a telephone call from a breathlessly urgent Tony Chester of Melton Mowbray, Leicestershire.

Tony was 'phoning from a vandalised public call-box a few yards from Wilstone Reservoir, Hertfordshire, where he had landed a tench which he reckoned was a record-breaker.

"It goes 10 lb. 2 oz. on two sets of scales—what's the present record?", he asked.

Here's the King of Tring, Melton Mowbray angler Tony Chester, with his 10 lb. 1¼ oz record tench, plus specimens of 7 lb 3 oz, 6 lb 15 oz and 5¼ lb.

I told him that according to the official records list he was a fraction of an ounce on the right side.

"Then you had better get over here quickly if you want a photograph. I've got the fish in the net", urged Tony.

That was good enough for me. I left reporter Beverly Adams to conduct a telephone interview with Tony while I organised transport, loaded cameras and headed through London's traffiic towards Tring.

An hour later I pulled into the pot-holed car park alongside Wilstone, one of the four well-known waters which make up the Tring group of reservoirs.

Wilstone is a huge area of water with a high, inhospitable concrete wall as the fishable bank. A small cluster of brollycamps could be seen to the right of the reservoir and I made my way towards them, little knowing that I was about to view the most prolific haul of heavyweight tench of all time.

Roy Ecob caught this 9 lb 7½ oz tench from Wilstone in the 1980 season.

Lester Strudwick (below) of Cuffley, Herts., with his Wilstone catch that included tench of 9 lb 3 oz, 5 lb 11 oz, 5 lb 6 oz and 5¼ lb.

In addition to Tony's 10-pounder, a 9 lb. 3 oz. tench, two 7-pounders, a couple of sixes and a number of fives had been taken by four anglers.

"Where's the lucky lad?", I enquired, as heads emerged from the bivouacs.

"Down in the village buying a bottle of whisky", explained Tony's fishing pal, Roy Ecob. "He needed something to calm his nerves!".

A few minutes later Tony returned, accompanied by his other fishing partner, Dick Wollaston, and they offered me a cuppa.

"While the kettle boils I'll tell you about the session that led up to the capture", suggested Tony and I tucked myself in his comfortable "bivvy", out of the unseasonal chill winds, and shared a tot of whisky as he put me in the picture.

"I have been fishing at Wilstone with Roy Ecob for two years and haven't had much luck. But just 24 hours into this season I broke my duck with a 7 lb. 3 oz. tench.

"That catch really bucked up my spirits and three hours later I hit another tench, which turned out to be the 10-pounder, hooked from a deep-water channel about 35 yards out".

Then Tony explained that his

Dick Wollaston with his fish of 7 lb 15 oz, 4 lb 14 oz and 3 lb 4 oz.

memorable catches had been made from a "second best" swim. The pitch he wanted was taken when he arrived at Tring, occupied by Lester Strudwick of nearby Cuffley, Hertfordshire.

But there were no hard feelings for Tony, Roy, Dick and Lester started to clock up what is probably the best heavyweight tench catch in angling history.

Their session started sluggishly but as the water temperature climbed the huge tench started to roll in a deep channel hotspot.

Tony had the 10 lb. 2 oz. specimen—later corrected to 10 lb. 1 oz. 4 dms. after scale checks by the Weights and Measures Office—plus others of 7 lb. 3 oz., 6 lb. 15 oz. and 5¼ lb.

In the next swim Lester Strudwick came close to the record with a giant tench of 9 lb. 3 oz., backed by specimens of 5 lb. 15 oz., 4 lb. 14 oz. and 3 lb. 4 oz.

Dick Wollaston netted tench of 7 lb. 15 oz., 4 lb. 14 oz. and 3¼ lb.

And Roy Ecob, the man who started the Tring ball rolling in the previous season with a beauty of 9 lb. 7½ oz., had another cracker of 6 lb. 9½ oz.

Tony's record-breaker fell for legered lobworm on a No. 4 hook to 6 lb. line, cast over a carpet of white bread crumb groundbait.

His bite of a lifetime came at 1.30 in the morning, a moment he will never forget.

"There was a normal, easy lift on my bite indictor and I hit it immediately and felt the fish kicking", he recalled.

"The tench put up a good fight for about four minutes and I thought it a lot smaller than it actually proved to be. My eyes popped when I saw it for the first time, it was so huge".

With my photographs taken and memories fresh of a group of delighted and dedicated anglers with a bag of tench I may never see again, I left the happy party to drink another toast to Tony's success and made my way back to the office in London to record in print and pictures what, for me, was the most exciting day of 1981 season.

TRING TICKETS

Day tickets cost £1 a day for Wilstone, Marsworth and Startops reservoirs in the Tring group. Juniors pay 50p. No Sunday fishing allowed. Tickets obtainable from bailiffs who patrol the bank from sunrise to sunset.

A Tring night syndicate, limited to 100 anglers, can fish at all times except on Sundays, for just over £30 a season.

For up-to-date details contact Tring bailiff, Bernard Double, telephone Tring (Herts) 2379.

d.i.y. BUILD YOUR OWN

TENCH fishing expert Len Head of Sudbury, Suffolk, shows in a step-by-step feature how to build your own personalised tench rod.

THE rod selected for this project is a fast-taper blank with a 1¼ lb test curve. It is ideal as a swimfeeder rod and will easily send a loaded feeder to the 70-yard mark and beyond. The fast taper also gives excellent line pick-up and direct contact with the fish on the strike at those distances. But it is not recommended as a general-purpose tench rod for which other blanks will be more suitable. the rod-building process is much the same, whatever the chosen blank.

THE KIT

1. An 11 ft 2 in fast-taper tench blank with 1¼ lb test curve; spigot already fitted.
2. Sixteen bored corks for handle (1½ in).
3. Fuji rod rings. Nine intermediates size 6, one butt ring size 12; model BMRFG.
4. Black anodised sliding reel fittings.
5. Rubber button 1¼ in. diameter.
6. Two reels of whipping thread No. 40.
7. Bottle Simpsons whipping dope No. 1 and bottle rod varnish No. 2.

Total approx cost incl. post and packing will be in the region of £30.
All materials supplied by Simpsons of Turnford, Broxbourne, Herts.

1

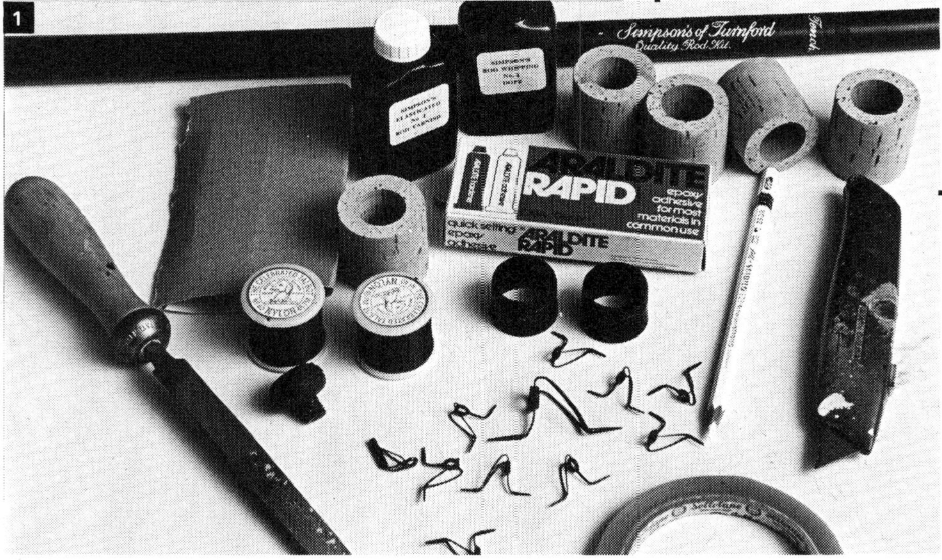

Basic materials required for building the rod: coarse file or Surform tool; reel of Sellotape; Stanley-knife; Araldite (glue); sandpaper (coarse, medium and fine grades); white wax pencil.

2

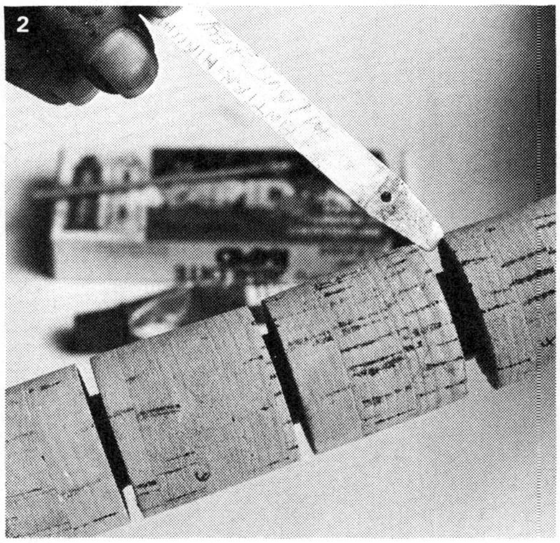

Begin by glueing the corks to the butt. Smear Araldite on to the blank then slide the corks over it, ensuring that plenty of glue is pushed between the corks. Glue and position only one cork at a time. Twist each cork as it is butted tightly on to the next, removing surplus glue if it is squeezed out. Use quick-drying Araldite "Rapid" which will allow shaping of the handle within an hour.

3

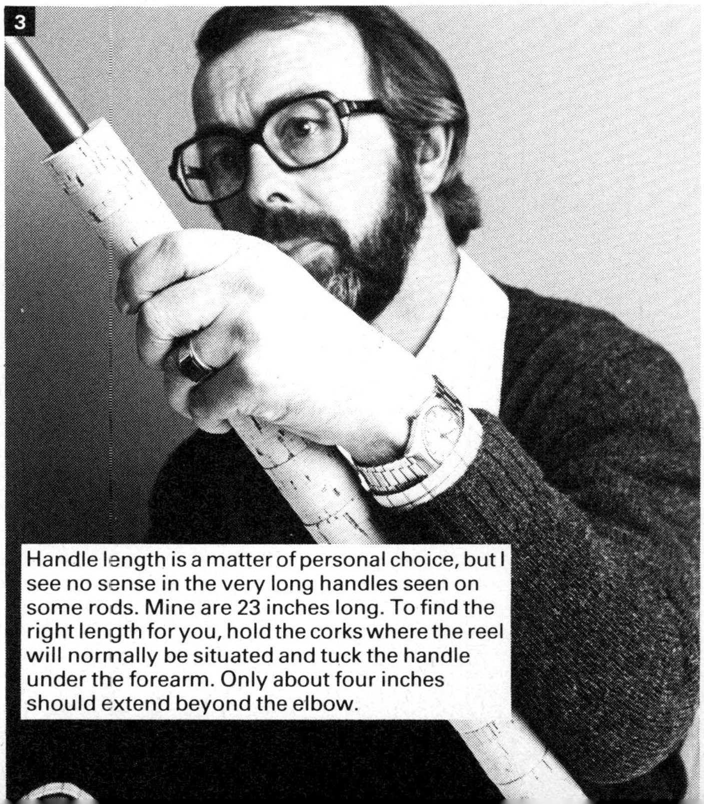

Handle length is a matter of personal choice, but I see no sense in the very long handles seen on some rods. Mine are 23 inches long. To find the right length for you, hold the corks where the reel will normally be situated and tuck the handle under the forearm. Only about four inches should extend beyond the elbow.

TENCH ROD

When the handle is dry, begin shaping corks, using coarse file or Surform tool. Work carefully and evenly down handle, ensuring that a uniform amount of shaping is done round. Mark lines at intervals down handle corks with lead pencil to help spot any bits missed. Test frequently for trueness by sighting down the handle as work progresses.

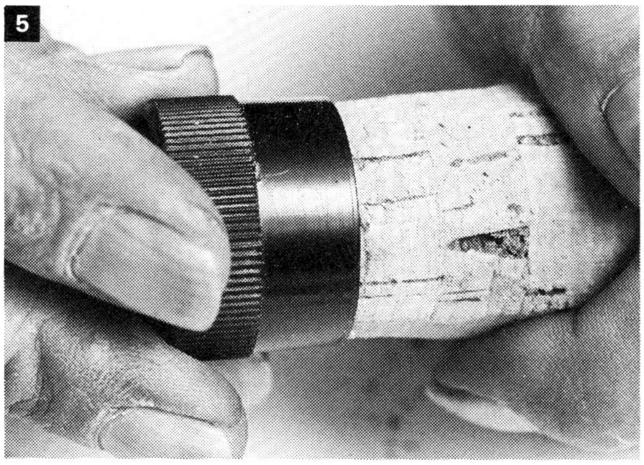

The sliding reel fitting should also be tested frequently for fit. Once the handle is completed the fittings need to be a good snug fit but able to slide freely with a little pressure.

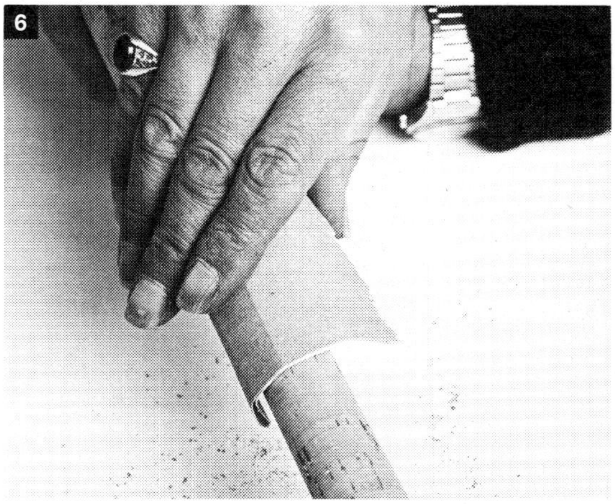

Having achieved a rough shape with the file, continue using the coarse sandpaper, then medium grade and finally fine grade until a smooth finish is obtained. While finishing with the find grade, save a little cork dust for later use.

I usually shape the top cork into a sort of cone as shown, but any shape of your choice can be made. When shaping curves such as a cone, make the job much easier by rolling a piece of sandpaper around a tube. Note the masking Sellotape around the rod above the corks to prevent accidental damage while shaping the end cork.

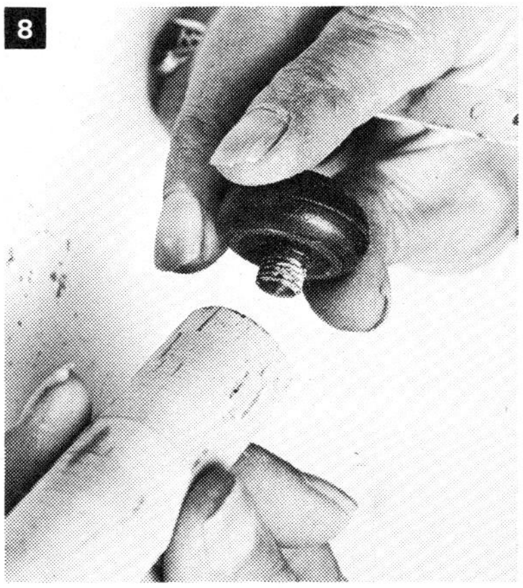

When the reel fittings are in position plug the open bottom end of the handle by glueing in a tight-fitting wine bottle cork. Then bore a hole in the middle of the cork and glue in the thread of the rubber button. Another way to finish the bottom of the handle is to leave off the last ten corks until the rest of the handle is shaped and the reel fittings are in position. Then glue on the corks you left off and sand to the required shape—usually slightly "bulbous" to prevent the reel fittings coming off. I favour the rubber button method as the handle can be completed in one stage instead of two.

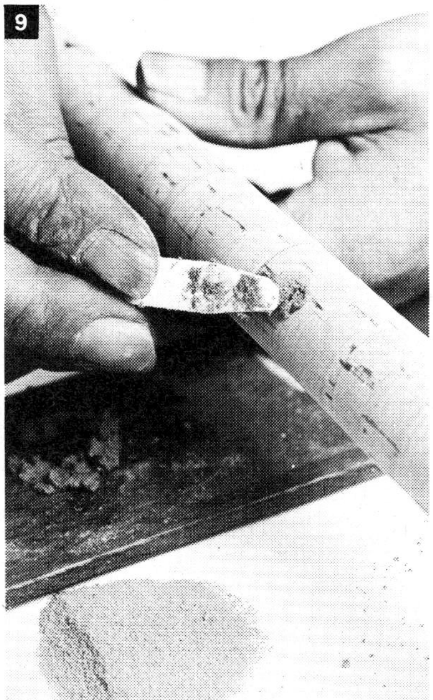

Mix the cork dust saved earlier with a little glue to make a filler paste. Use this to fill any holes or imperfections in the cork, finally smoothing off when dry.

10

Many blanks will be seen to have a slight natural curve at the tip when sighted along the rod as shown. The rod rings should always be fixed to the *outside* bend of any such curve. The weight of the rings will counteract the curve and should result in a dead straight tip once they are whipped in place.

11

When the presence of any tip curve has been established, as described, mark both sections of the blank on the line where the rings are to be fixed. A white wax pencil is useful for temporary marking of the blank as the mark is easily erased later. These pencils are available from art shops. Ask for a "Stabilo" pencil.

12
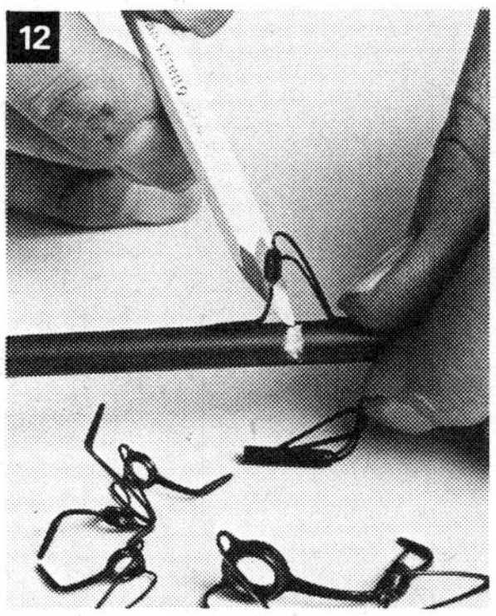

Next step is to mark the blank where each of the rings are to go. The ring spacings on this particular rod, measuring from the tip are: 4 in, 5 in, 6 in. 7 in. 8½ in. 12 in. 13½ in. 16 in. and 17 in. Be careful not to put the rings on backwards! Note the shape of the Fujis and the way they are fitted to the rod—the tip of the rod is on the left of the picture.

13

A smooth whipping with no "step" at the foot of the rings, can be achieved by filing each ring-foot to a smooth flat taper.

14

IT makes no great difference whether you begin whipping-on the rings at the tip or the butt, but I usually begin with the butt ring. Position it on the rod as required, using a piece of Sellotape on one foot.

16
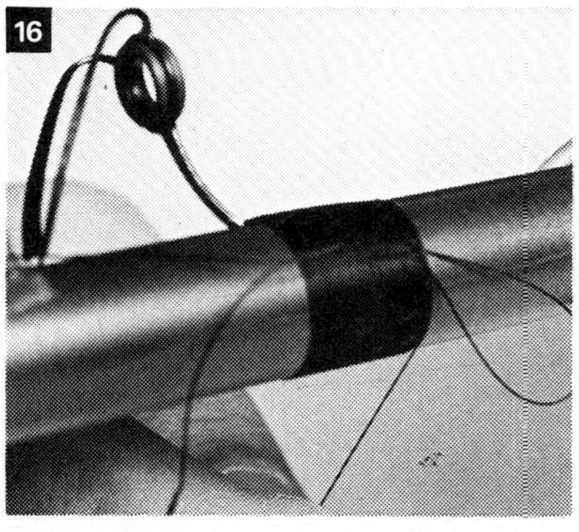

Finish off the whipping, by inserting a spare loop of thread as shown. Continue whipping for another six turns over the loop. Cut the whipping thread and poke the end through the "eye" of the loop, then pull the loop by its free ends back through the six turns, causing the cut end of the whipping thread to follow it through. Trim the loose end closely with a sharp blade. Remove the Sellotape from the other foot, adjust the ring for trueness if necessary, then complete the other whipping. Continue with the rest of the rings, checking frequently each one for straightness with those already completed.

15
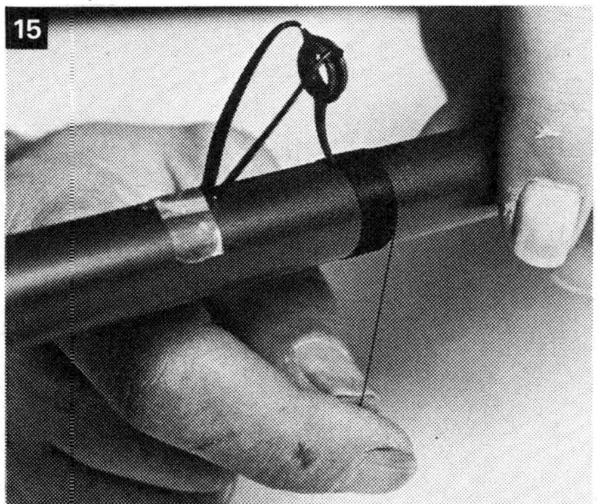

ALWAYS whip down the foot of the ring, never up it. If you whip upwards it is difficult to avoid that "step" as you reach the foot, no matter how carefully you tapered it. Don't try to wind the thread around the rod, just hold it under slight pressure with one hand while the rod is rotated with the other hand.

17
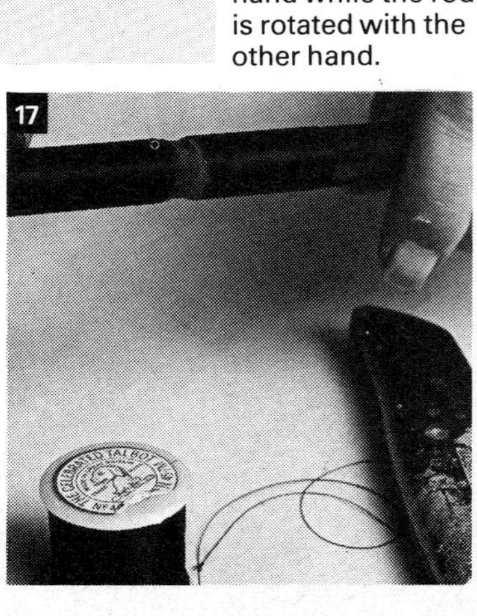

When the intermediate rings are in place whip either side of the spigot joints, as shown, for at least 1½ in. These joints are subjected to a lot of stress, especially when casting heavy feeders, and the whipping adds strength. Run a thumbnail along the whippings, including those holding the rings. This smooths out and closes up any little gaps which may have been left.

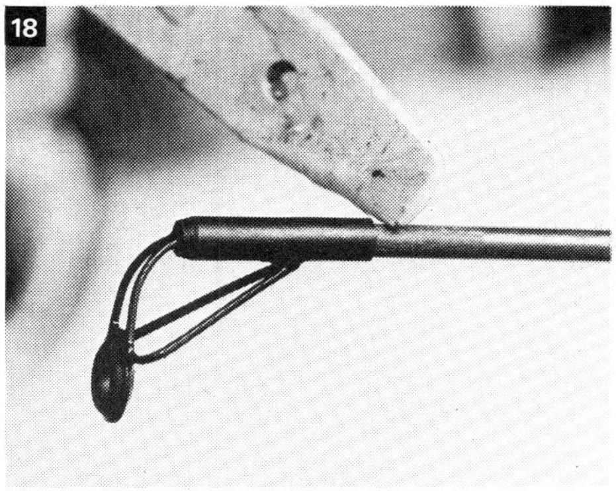

Glue on the tip ring, ensuring it is in line with the intermediate rings. It is not necessary, but looks better if a short whipping is done below and buffing up to the tip ring.

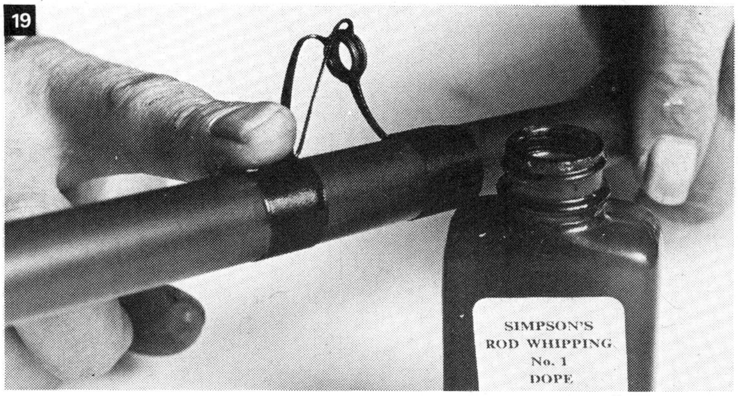

Rub dope No. 1 into the whipping with the fingertip. At least three applications are needed to really seal and stick the rings firmly to the rod.

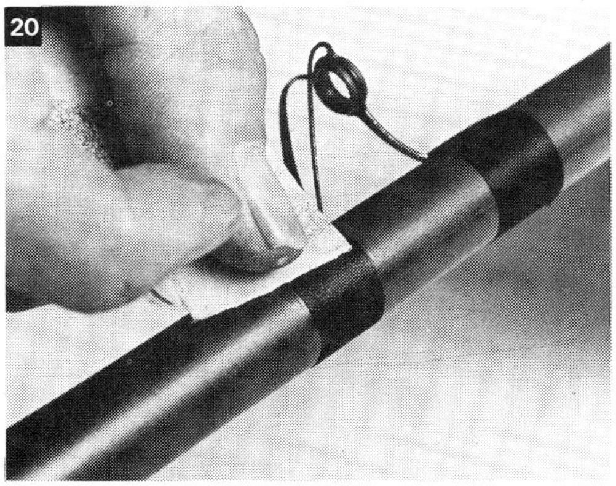

When the first coat of dope is thoroughly dry—and don't risk it before—smooth off any fluffyness from the whipping thread by using the finest sandpaper. Care at this stage will ensure a good finish later.

Varnish all the whippings, using rod varnish No. 2. One coat will do but several will ensure a quality finish.

No. 2 varnish is used to varnish the whole rod. Apply two or three coats in a dust-free atmosphere with a fine bristle brush such as ox-hair, spreading varnish in even thin coats, ensuring each coat dries for at least 24 hours before applying the next.

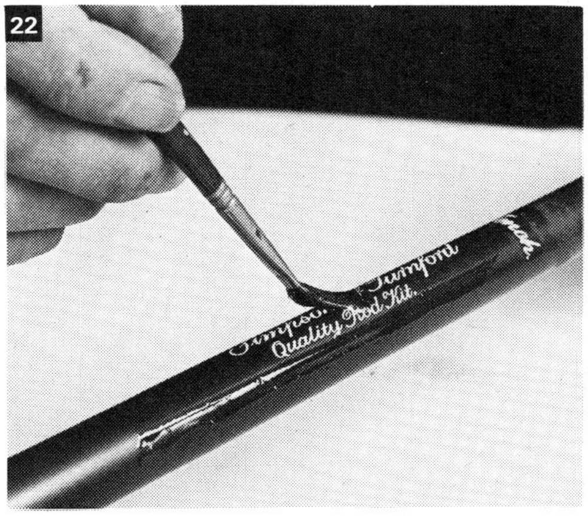

Personalising the rod with your name adds a finishing touch and is a deterrent against light fingers. If not "arty" enough to do it freehand, "Letraset" from office supply shops does the job equally well, if not better. Best done before the final varnish coat is applied.

A non-essential finishing touch but one which saves time at the waterside is to paint on a couple of level dots on the top and bottom sections, either side of the spigot joint. When setting up the rod simply line up the dots, which avoids peering along the rod to see if the rings are lined up. Now your rod is finished and all that remains is for me to wish you lots of tench using it!

BRITISH RECORD FISH LIST

Tony Chester, of Melton Mowbray, set a cracking pace in the 1981 coarse season with this superb 10 lb 1 oz 4 dms tench. Full story and more pictures in pages 45 to 47.

Recognised as at March 1982

SEA FISH (Boat Records)

	Weight lb.	oz.	dr. :	kilo.	grms.	Captor and Venue	Date
Angler Fish	82	12	0 :	37	533	K. Ponsford, Mevagissey, Cornwall	1977
Bass	18	6	0 :	8	334	R. G. Slater, off Eddystone Reef, Plymouth	1975
Black-fish	3	10	8 :	1	658	James Semple, off Head of Ayr, Scotland	1972
Bluemouth	3	2	8 :	1	431	Anne Lyneham, Loch Shell, Stornoway	1976
Bogue	**1**	**13**	**0 :**	**0**	**822**	**K. McBride, Eddystone Reef**	**1981**
Bream, Black	6	14	4 :	3	118	J. Garlick (Torquay), Wreck off Devon coast	1977
Bream, Gilthead	5	0	0 :	2	268	A. H. Stratton-Knott, off St. Mawes, Cornwall	1978
Bream, Ray's	6	3	13 :	2	829	J. Holland, Barra Head, Scotland	1978
Bream, Red	9	8	12 :	4	330	B. H. Reynolds, off Mevagissey, Cornwall	1974
Brill	16	0	0 :	7	257	A. H. Fisher, Isle of Man	1950
Bull Huss	21	3	0 :	9	610	J. Holmes, Looe, Cornwall	1955
Catfish	24	3	0 :	10	999	N. Trevelyan, Whitby, Yorks	1980
Coalfish	33	7	0 :	15	155	L. M. Saunders, off Stone Point, Devon	1980
Cod	53	0	0 :	24	039	G. Martin, Start Point, Devon	1972
Comber	1	13	0 :	0	822	B. Phillips, Mounts Bay, Cornwall	1977
Common Skate	226	8	0 :	102	733	R. S. Macpherson, Duny Voe, Shetland	1970
Conger	109	6	0 :	49	607	R. W. Potter, S.E. of Eddystone, Plymouth	1976
Dab	2	12	4 :	1	254	R. Islip, Gairloch, Wester Ross, Scotland	1975
Dogfish, Black-Mouthed	2	13	8 :	1	288	J. H. Anderson, Loch Fyne, Scotland	1977
Dogfish, Lesser Spotted	4	1	13 :	1	863	B. J. Solomon, Newquay, Cornwall	1976
Flounder	5	11	8 :	2	593	A. G. L. Cobbledick, Fowey, Cornwall	1956
Forkbeard, Greater	4	11	4 :	2	133	Miss M. Woodgate, Falmouth Bay, Cornwall	1969
Garfish	**3**	**0**	**2 :**	**1**	**363**	**J. Nardini, Penzance**	**1981**
Greater Weever	2	4	0 :	1	020	P. Ainslie, Brighton	1927
Gurnard, Grey	2	7	0 :	1	104	D. Swinbanks, Caliach Point, Mull, Scotland	1976

Sea Fish (Boats) Records, continued

	Weight						
	lb.	oz.	dr. :	kilo.	grms.	Captor and Venue	Date
Gurnard, Red	5	0	0 :	2	268	B. D. Critchley, off Rhyl, Wales	1973
Gurnard, Streaked	0	12	0 :	0	340	Qualifying weight	—
Gurnard, Yellow or Tubfish	11	7	4 :	5	195	C. W. King, Wallasey, Cheshire	1952
Haddock	13	11	4 :	6	215	G. Bones, off, Falmouth, Cornwall	1978
Haddock, Norway	1	13	8 :	0	836	T. Barrett, off Southend	1975
Hake	25	5	8 :	11	494	H. W. Steele, Belfast Lough, Nth Ireland	1962
Halibut	234	0	0 :	106	136	C. Booth, Dunnet Head, Thurso, Scotland	1979
Herring	1	1	0 :	0	481	Brett Barden, off Bexhill, Sussex	1973
John Dory	11	14	0 :	5	386	J. Johnson, Newhaven, Sussex	1977
Ling	57	2	8 :	25	924	H. Solomons, off Mevagissey, Cornwall	1975
Lumpsucker	10	12	0 :	4	872	D. W. Jordan, off Shoreham, Sussex	1980
Mackerel	5	6	8 :	2	452	S. Beasley, Eddystone, Devon	1969
Megrim	3	12	8 :	1	714	P. Christie, Loch Gairloch, Scotland	1973
Monkfish	66	0	0 :	29	936	C. G. Chalk, Shoreham, Sussex	1965
Mullet, Golden Grey	**1**	**14**	**4 :**	**0**	**857**	**R. Smith, Falmouth**	**1981**
Mullet, Red	**3**	**7**	**0 :**	**1**	**559**	**M. Hamel, Vale, Guernsey, C.I.**	**1981**
Mullet, Thick-Lipped Grey	10	1	0 :	4	564	P. C. Libby, Portland, Dorset	1952
Mullet, Thin-Lipped Grey	**2**	**9**	**8 :**	**1**	**176**	**I. Williams (7), Christchurch**	**1981**
	2	**9**	**8 :**	**1**	**176**	**T. Quinn, Christchurch**	**1981**
Opah	128	0	0 :	58	057	A. R. Blewett, Mounts Bay, Penzance	1973
Pelamid, (Bonito)	8	13	4 :	4	004	J. Parnell, Torbay, Devon	1969
Perch, Dusky	28	0	0 :	12	700	D. Cope, off Durlston Head, Dorset	1973
Plaice	10	3	8 :	4	624	H. Gardiner, Longasound, Scotland	1974
Pollack	25	0	12 :	11	550	R. J. Vines, off Teignmouth	1980
Pouting (Bib, Pout)	5	8	0 :	2	494	R. S. Armstrong, off Berry Head, Devon	1969
Ray, Blonde	37	12	0 :	17	122	H. T. Pout, off Start Point, Devon	1973
Ray, Bottle-nosed	76	0	0 :	34	471	R. Bulpitt, off Needles, Isle of Wight	1970
Ray, Cuckoo	5	11	0 :	2	579	V. Morrison, off Causeway C.I.	1975
Ray, Eagle	52	8	0 :	23	812	R. J. Smith, off Nab Tower, Isle of Wight	1972
Ray, Electric	96	1	0 :	43	571	N. J. Cowley, off Dodman Point, Cornwall	1975
Ray, Sandy	2	0	0 :	0	910	Qualifying weight	—
Ray, Small-eyed	16	4	0 :	7	370	H. T. Pout, Salcombe, Devon	1973
Ray, Spotted	6	14	0 :	3	118	H. A. Jamieson, off Causeway Coast, NI	1978
Ray, Sting	61	8	0 :	27	894	V. W. Roberts, Pwllheli, Gwyneth	1979
Ray, Thornback	38	0	0 :	17	236	J. Patterson, Rustington, Sussex	1935
Ray, Undulate	19	6	13 :	8	811	L. R. Le Page, Herm, Channel Islands	1970
Rockling, 3-bearded	3	2	0 :	1	424	N. Docksey, Portland, Breakwater, Dorset	1976
Rockling, Shore	1	0	0 :	0	454	Qualifying weight	—
Salmon, Coho	1	0	0 :	0	454	Qualifying weight	—
Sea-scorpion, Short-spined	2	3	0 :	0	992	R. Stephenson, Gt. Cumbrae Island, Scotland	1976
Scad (Horse Mackerel)	3	5	3 :	1	507	M. A. Atkins, Torbay, Devon	1978
Shad, Allis	2	0	0 :	0	910	Qualifying weight	—
Shad, Twaite	(3	2	0 :	1	417)	T. Hayward, Deal	1949
	(3	2	0 :	1	417)	S. Jenkins, Torbay	1954
Shark, Blue	218	0	0 :	98	878	N. Sutcliffe, Looe, Cornwall	1959
Shark, Mako	500	0	0 :	226	786	Mrs. J. M. Yallop, off Eddystone, Devon	1971
Shark, Porbeagle	465	0	0 :	210	911	J. Potier, off Padstow, Cornwall	1976
Shark, Thresher	295	0	0 :	133	804	H. J. Aris, Dunose Head, I.o.W.	1978
Shark, Six-Gilled	9	8	0 ;	4	308	F. E. Beeton, Penlee Point, Plymouth	1976
Smoothhound, Starry	28	0	0 :	12	700	R. Grady, Maplin Sands, Essex	1980
Smoothhound	28	0	0 :	12	700	A. T. Chilvers, Heacham, Norfolk	1969
Sole	3	12	4 :	1	708	S. Brice, Fishbourn Creek, IOW	1980
Sole, Lemon	2	2	0 :	0	963	**J. Gordon, Loch Goil Head, Scotland**	**1976**
Spanish Mackerel	1	0	6 :	0	464	P. Jones, off Guernsey, C.I.	1972
Spurdog	21	3	7 :	9	624	P. Barrett, Porthleven, Cornwall	1977
Sunfish	108	0	0 :	48	986	T. F. Sisson, Saundersfoot, Pembs., Wales	1976
Tadpole fish	**0**	**14**	**14 :**	**0**	**421**	**R. Donnelly, Lunderston Bay, Renfrewshire**	**1981**
Tope	74	11	0 :	33	876	A. S. Harries, Caldy Island	1964
Torsk	12	1	0 :	5	471	D. Pottinger, Shetland	1968
Trigger Fish	4	9	5 :	2	077	E. Montacute, Weymouth	1975
Tunny	851	0	0 :	385	989	L. Mitchell Henry, Whitby, Yorks	1933
Turbot	33	12	0 :	15	308	R. Simcox, Kingsbridge, Devon	1980
Witch	0	12	0 :	0	340	Qualifying weight	—
Whiting	6	4	0 :	2	834	S. Dearman, West Bay, Bridport, Dorset	1977
Whiting, Blue (Poutassou)	1	12	0 :	0	793	J. H. Anderson, Loch Fyne, Scotland	1977
Wrasse, Ballan	**9**	**6**	**0 :**	**4**	**252**	**M. Goodacre, Eddystone Gully**	**1981**
Wrasse, Cuckoo	2	0	8 :	0	921	A. M. Foley, off Plymouth	1973
Wreck Fish	10	10	0 :	4	819	B. McNamara, S. of Eddystone Reef	1980

SEA FISH (Shore Records)

	Weight						
	lb.	oz.	dr. :	kilo.	grms.	Captor and Venue	Date
Angler Fish	68	2	0 :	30	899	J. G. T. Legerton, Canvey Island, Essex	1967
Bass	18	2	0 :	8	220	F. C. Borley, Felixstowe, Suffolk	1943
Black-fish	1	0	0 :	0	453	Qualifying weight	—
Bluemouth	1	0	0 :	0	453	Quailfying weight	—
Bogue	1	15	4 :	0	885	S. G. Torode, Pembroke, Guernsey, C.I.	1978
Bream, Black	4	14	4 :	2	217	R. J. Holloway, Admiralty Pier, Dover	1977
Bream, Gilthead	6	15	0 :	3	146	H. Solomons, Salcombe Estuary, Devon	1977

	Weight						
	lb.	oz.	dr. :	kilo.	grms.	Captor and Venue	Date
Bream, Ray's	7	15	12 :	3	621	G. Walker, Crimdon Beach, Hartlepool	1967
Bream, Red	4	7	0 :	2	026	A. Salmon, Alderney, C.I.	1979
Brill	7	7	8 :	3	387	B. M. K. Fletcher, Guernsey, C.I.	1980
Bull Huss	17	15	0 :	8	135	M. Roberts, Falmouth	1977
Catfish	12	12	8 :	5	797	G. M. Taylor, Stonehaven, Scotland	1978
Coalfish	18	0	0 :	8	164	B. Hill, Ilfracombe	1979
Cod	44	8	0 :	20	183	B. Jones, Toms Points, Barry, Glam.	1966
Comber	0	12	0 :	0	340	Qualifying weight	—
Common Skate	100	0	0 :	45	357	Qualifying weight	—
Conger	67	1	0 :	30	418	A. W. Lander, Arch Rock End, Torquay	1977
Dab	2	9	8 :	1	176	M. L. Watts, Port Talbot, Wales	1936
Dogfish, Black-Mouthed	0	12	0 :	0	340	Qualifying weight	—
Dogfish, Lesser Spotted	4	8	0 :	2	040	J. Beattie, off Ayr Pier, Scotland	1969
Flounder	5	2	0 :	2	324	W. Stevens, Teign Estuary, Devon	1978
Forkbeard, Greater	1	0	0 :	0	453	Qualifying weight	—
Garfish	2	15	9 :	1	347	M. Wills, Coverack, Cornwall	1979
Greater Weever	1	4	11 :	0	586	N. Hall, St. Agnes, Cornwall	1980
Gurnard, Grey	1	8	0 :	0	680	S. Quine, Isle of Man	1977
Gurnard, Red	2	10	11 :	1	435	D. Johns, Helford River, Cornwall	1976
Gurnard, Streaked	1	6	8 :	0	637	H. Livingstone Smith, Loch Goil, Firth of Clyde	1971
Gurnard, Yellow or Tubfish	12	3	0 :	5	527	G. J. Reynolds, Langland Bay, Wales	1976
Haddock	6	12	0 :	3	061	G. B. Stevenson, Loch Goil, Firth of Clyde	1976
Haddock, Norway	1	3	0 :	0	538	F. P. Fawke, Southend Pier, Essex	1973
Hake	2	8	8 :	**1**	**148**	**W. May, The Lizard, Cornwall**	**1981**
Halibut	10	0	0 :	4	540	Qualifying weight	—
Herring	1	0	0 :	0	454	Qualifying weight	—
John Dory	3	0	0 :	1	360	Qualifying weight	—
Ling	**19**	**4**	0 :	8	731	D. J. Rogan, SW coast of Jersey, C.I.	1981
Lumpsucker	14	3	0 :	6	435	W. J. Burgess, off Felixstowe Beach, Suffolk	1970
Mackerel	4	0	8 :	1	828	P. Porter, Breakwater, Peel, Isle of Man	1952
Megrim	1	0	0 :	0	453	Qualifying weight	—
Monkfish	50	0	0 :	22	679	Qualifying weight	—
Mullet, Golden Grey	2	10	0 :	1	190	R. J. Hopkins, Burry Port, Llanelli, Wales	1976
Mullet, Red	3	10	0 :	1	644	J. E. Martell, Guernsey, C.I.	1967
Mullet, Thick-Lipped Grey	14	2	12 :	6	427	R. Gifford, Aberthaw, Glam.	1979
Mullet, Thin-Lipped Grey	**6**	**4**	**0 :**	**2**	**835**	**H. Mepham, River Rother, Sussex**	**1981**

Keith McBride, of Doncaster, with the 2 lb 2 oz record bogue which he caught from Plymouth, Devon.

Ragworm bait tempted this 1 lb 14 oz golden grey mullet for Falmouth, Cornwall, youngster Robin Smith. The fish beats the previous best from a boat by just five drams.

	Weight lb.	oz.	dr. :	kilo.	grms.	Captor and Venue	Date
Opah	20	0	0 :	9	071	Qualifying weight	—
Pelamid, (Bonito)	2	0	0 :	0	910	Qualifying weight	—
Perch, Dusky	7	0	0 :	3	175	Qualifying weight	—
Plaice	8	1	4 :	3	663	N. Mills, Southend Pier, Essex	1976
Pollack	16	0	0 :	7	257	B. Raybould, Portland Bill, Dorset	1977
Pouting (Bib, Pout)	3	4	0 :	1	474	P. T. Weekes, Dover Breakwater	1978
Ray, Blonde	30	4	0 :	13	720	J. T. Lowe, Nth Coast, Jersey, C.I.	1980
Ray, Bottle-nosed	15	0	0 :	6	800	Qualifying weight	—
Ray, Cuckoo	4	8	11 :	2	060	W. Robb, Skelmorlie, Ayrshire	1979
Ray, Eagle	15	0	0 :	6	800	Qualifying weight	—
Ray, Electric	52	11	0 :	24	029	M. A. Wills, Porthallow, Cornwall	1980
Ray, Sandy	4	0	0 :	1	814	Qualifying weight	—
Ray, Small-eyed	**14**	**2**	**11 :**	**6**	**426**	**T. Martinez, Trevose Head, Cornwall**	**1981**
Ray, Spotted	8	5	0 :	3	770	D. Bowen, Gower Peninsular, Wales	1980
Ray, Sting	51	4	0 :	23	245	A. L. Stevens, Sowley Beach, Hants	1975
Ray, Thornback	21	0	0 :	9	525	R. Brown, Balcary Point, Auchencairn, Scotland	1980
Ray, Undulate	17	12	0 :	8	051	K. Skinner, St. Catherine's Breakwater, Jersey	1979
Rockling, 3-bearded	2	14	10 :	1	321	P. Cottell, Dart Estuary, Devon	1980
Rockling, Shore	1	1	4 :	0	488	A. Bayes, Gristhorpe, Scarborough	1976
Salmon, Coho	1	8	1 :	0	681	R. J. McCracken, St. Sampsons, Guernsey, C.I.	1977
Sea-scorpion, (Short-spined)	**2**	**7**	**8 :**	**1**	**119**	**B. Logan, Whitley Bay, Tyne & Wear**	**1981**
Scad (Horse Mackerel)	**3**	**0**	**14 :**	**1**	**385**	**R. Dillon, Cockenzie, Scotland**	**1981**
Shad, Allis	4	12	7 :	2	168	P. Gerrard, Chesil Beach, Dorset	1977
Shad, Twaite	2	12	0 :	1	247	J. W. Martin, Garlieston, Wigtownshire, Scotland	1978
Shark, Blue	40	0	0 :	18	140	Qualifying weight	—
Shark, Mako	40	0	0 :	18	140	Qualifying weight	—
Shark, Porbeagle	40	0	0 :	18	140	Qualifying weight	—
Shark, Thresher	40	0	0 :	18	140	Qualifying weight	—
Smoothhound, Starry	23	2	0 :	10	488	D. Carpenter, Beach, Bradwell-on-Sea, Essex	1972
Smoothhound	**15**	**12**	**12 :**	**7**	**165**	**G. E. Jones, Boverton, Glam.**	**1981**
Sole	5	7	1 :	2	467	L. Dixon, Sth Coast, Alderney, C.I.	1980
Sole, Lemon	2	7	11 :	1	124	W. N. Callister, Douglas, I.O.M.	1980
Spanish Mackerel	0	12	0 :	0	340	Qualifying weight	—
Spurdog	16	12	8 :	7	611	R. Legg, Chesil Beach, Dorset	1964
Sunfish	49	4	0 :	22	338	M. Merry, North Cliffs, Cornwall	1976
Tadpole fish	1	3	12 :	0	595	D. Higgins, Whitley Bay, Tyne and Wear	1977
Tope	54	4	0 :	24	606	D. Hastings, Loch Ryan, Wigtownshire, Scotland	1975
Torsk	3	0	0 :	1	360	Qualifying weight	—
Trigger Fish	4	6	0 :	1	984	M. J. Blew, Bossington Beach, Somerset	1975
Tunny	40	0	0 :	18	140	Qualifying weight	—
Turbot	28	8	0 :	12	926	J. D. Dorling, Dunwich Beach, Suffolk	1973
Witch	1	2	13 :	0	533	T. J. Barathy, Colwyn Bay, Wales	1967
Whiting, Blue (Poutassou)	0	12	0 :	0	340	L. Peters, Abbotsbury Beach, Dorset	1978
Wrasse, Ballan	8	6	6 :	3	808	R. W. LePage, Bordeaux Beach, Guernsey, C.I.	1976
Wrasse, Cuckoo	1	9	4 :	0	715	D. Rohdich, Causeway Coast, N.I.	1979
Wreck Fish	1	0	0 :	0	453	Qualifying weight	—

Mini sea records

	Weight oz.	dr. : grms.	Captor and Venue	Date
Anchovy	1	8 : 042	R. H. Wilcox, Port Talbot	1979
Argentine	5	3 : 147	I. Millar, Loch Long, Scotland	1978
Blenny, Tompot	5	2 : 144	J. Hughes, Portland Bill, Dorset	1977
Blenny, Viviparous	12	2 : 343	N. Kirk, Redcar beach, Cleveland	1979
Blenny, Yarrell's	2	1 : 059	D. McEntee, Gourock Pier, Clyde	1979
Butterfish	1	2 : 032	D. McEntee, Gourock Pier, Clyde	1978
Dab, Long Rough	5	8 : 155	I. McGrath, Coulport, Loch Long, Scotland	1975
Dragonet	5	8 : 155	R. J. F. Pearce, Berry Head Quarry, Devon	1980
Goby, Black	**2**	**1 : 058**	**N. Molyneux, Pembroke Dock**	**1981**
Goby, Giant	6	10 : 187	P. A. Cadogan, Herm Is., Nr. Guernsey, C.I.	1974
Goby, Rock	1	0 : 029	D. McEntee, Penlee Point, Devon	1979
Greater Pipefish	4	0 : 113	T. J. Sherwood, Portsmouth Harbour	1981
Pilchard	7	0 : 198	K. W. Jarrett, Littlehampton, Sussex	1976
Pogge	0	10 : 018	R. Owen, Aberffraw	1979
Poor Cod	10	5 : 294	H. Livingston Smith, Gantocks, Scotland	1976
Poutassou	9	8 : 269	N. Hunt, off Falmouth, Cornwall	1972
Red Band Fish	6	4 : 180	L. K. Bradbury, off Paignton, Devon	1975
Rockling, Five-Bearded	9	4 : 262	P. R. Winder, Lancing Beach, Sussex	1968
Rockling, Four-Bearded	**1**	**7 : 040**	**S. Hodgson, Cloch Point, Renfrewshire**	**1981**
Sandeel, Corbin's	4	9 : 129	S. L. Carter, NW of Jersey, C.I.	1978
Sandeel, Greater	8	7 : 239	B. K. Le Breton, Herm, Guernsey, C.I.	1979
Sea Scorpion (Long-spined)	8	0 : 226	W. Crone, Plymouth	1978
Shanny	2	6 : 068	D. McEntee, St. Penlee Point, Devon	1979
Smelt	6	12 : 191	G. Idiens, Fleetwood, Lancs	1981
Smelt, Sand	2	9 : 072	A. D. Laws. St. Peter Port, Guernsey, C.I.	1975
Smelt, Sand (Big-scale)	0	5 : 008	N. L. G. Dorling, The Leys, Aberthaw, Wales	1980
Stickleback, Sea	0	4 : 007	K. Pilley, Poole Harbour, Dorset	1978
Topknot, Common	11	2 : 315	P. Andrews, St. Catherines, Jersey, C.I.	1972
Weever, Lesser	2	2 : 060	M. Nickolls, Schole Bank, off Guernsey, C.I.	1976
Wrasse, Corkwing	11	4 : 318	T. R. Woodman, off Portland Bill, Dorset	1974
Wrasse, Goldsinny	2	12 : 079	M. Sansom, Portland Bill, Dorset	1980
Wrasse, Rock Cook	2	11 : 077	J. Sansom, Portland Bill, Dorset	1980

FRESHWATER FISH

	Weight lb.	oz.	dr. :	kilo.	grms.	Captor and Venue	Date
Barbel	13	12	0 :	6	237	J. Day, Hampshire Avon	1962
Bleak	0	3	15:	0	111	D. Pollard, Staythorpe Pond, Nr, Newark, Notts	1971
Bream (Common, Bronze)	13	8	0 :	6	123	A. R. Heslop, private water in Staffordshire	1977
Bullhead, (Millers Thumb)	0	0	12 :	0	021	E. Whalley, Small Stream at Cawthorne, Yorks.	1981
*Carp	44	0	0 :	19	975	R. Walker, Redmire Pool	1952
Carp, Crucian	5	10	8 :	2	565	G. Halls, Lakes, Kings Lynn, Norfolk	1976
Catfish, (Wels)	43	8	0 :	19	730	R. J. Bray, Wilstone Reservoir, Tring, Herts.	1970
Char	1	12	4 :	0	801	C. Imperiale, Loch Insh, Inverness-shire	1974
Chub	7	6	0 :	3	345	W. L. Warren, Hampshire Avon	1957
Dace	1	4	4 :	0	574	J. L. Gasson, Little Ouse, Thetford, Norfolk	1960
Eel	11	2	0 :	5	046	S. Terry, Kingfisher Lake, Nr. Ringwood, Hants	1978
Grayling	2	13	0 :	1	275	P. B. Goldsmith, River Test, Romsey	1981
Gudgeon	0	4	8 :	0	127	J. R. Hack, River Clweddg, Wrexham	1981
Gwyniad (Whitefish)	1	4	0 :	0	567	J. R. Williams, Llyn Tegid, Wales	1965
Loch Lomond Powan	1	7	0 :	0	652	J. M. Ryder, Loch Lomond, Scotland	1972
Minnow	0	0	13 :	0	023	R. Merrifield, River Calder, Lancs	1981
Orfe, Golden	4	3	0 :	1	899	B. T. Mills, River Test, Hampshire	1976
Perch	4	12	0 :	2	154	S. F. Baker, Oulton Broad	1962
Pike	40	0	0 :	18	143	P. D. Hancock, Horsey Mere, Norfolk	1967
Pike-perch (Walleye)	11	12	0 :	5	329	F. Adams, Delph, Welney, Cambs	1934
Pike-perch (Zander)	17	4	0 :	7	828	D. Litton, Gt. Ouse, Relief Channel	1977
Pumpkinseed	0	2	10 :	0	074	A. Baverstock, GLC Highgate Pond, London	1977
Roach	4	1	0 :	1	842	R. G. Jones, Notts, gravel pit	1975
*Rudd	4	8	0 :	2	041	Rev. E. C. Alston, Thetford, Norfolk	1933
Ruffe	0	5	4 :	0	148	R. J. Jenkins, West View Farm, Cumbria	1980
*Salmon	64	0	0 :	29	029	Miss G. W. Ballantyne, River Tay, Scotland	1922
Schelly (Skelly)	1	10	0 :	0	737	W. Wainwright, Ullswater, Cumbria	1976
Tench	10	1	4 :	4	571	A. J. Chester, Wilstone Reservoir, Tring, Herts	1981
Trout, American Brook (Brook Char)	5	13	8 :	2	650	A. Pearson, Avington Fishery, Hants	1981
Trout, Brown	19	9	4 :	8	880	A. Jackson, Loch Quoish, Inverness-shire	1978
Trout, Rainbow	19	8	0 :	8	844	A. Pearson, Avington Fishery, Hants	1977

*Denotes the fish for which the cast or body was available for inspection: Caught before the formation of the Committee.

Species open for freshwater fish claims (Minimum qualifying weights). **Sea Trout** (15 lb.). **Silver Bream** (1lb) Qualifying weights are subject to revision by the Committee if necessary.

• *The Editor wishes to thank Mr. Peter Tombleson and the Britisn Record (rod caught) Fish Committee for their assistance in compiling these lists.*

WHAT, WHERE, WHEN, HOW?

DO you know how to tell the difference between a small chub and a big dace . . . a pollack and a coalfish . . . or a hybrid from a true roach? Do you know the current official record targets of, at least, the most popular freshwater and sea species?

If still saying "yes", do you know what to do and whom to contact, if the great day comes when the biggest fish of its kind ever caught on rod and line could win you a memorable place in Britain's angling roll of honour?

Surprisingly few anglers, including some dedicated to the art of specimen hunting, are really boned-up on the procedure to follow when staking a claim to a record. A false move at that vital stage could wreck a chance that may never come again.

Correct identification of the catch is one of the priorities. That is one of the reasons why the Records Committee insists no claim will be considered unless the fish in its natural state (dead or alive) is available for inspection by someone acting for the Committee.

So the first thing to do is **KEEP THE FISH** and contact the Secretary of the British (rod-caught) Records Committee immediately. His telephone number and address are shown below and should be in a notebook in your tackle box at all times. Use the notebook to record the names, addresses and telephone numbers (if any) of reliable independent witnesses of the weight and capture. They will be asked to sign forms supporting your claim.

Then put in a written claim, stating species, weight, date and place of capture, tackle used, whether caught from boat or shore (sea fish records are listed in separate sections) and details of your witnesses.

Fish caught from a boat at sea are eligible for consideration if the boat used sets out from a port in England, Wales, Scotland, Northern Ireland, Isle of Man or Channel Islands and returns to a UK port without calling at any port outside the UK. Catches made in the territorial waters of other countries are out.

Shore fishing is defined officially as fishing from any land mass of fixed man-made structure.

If in any doubt, the Committee Secretary will settle queries and can also brief you on how to preserve the fish for inspection.

Next important step—telephone Angler's Mail Newsdesk; the charge can be reversed and the News Editor's direct telephone numbers appear every week in Angler's Mail. Tell him what you've caught, where you are and if photos are available—or if your fish can be photographed by his local photographer. The News Editor can also tell you the latest official record weight of any fish in the official lists—if there's a doubt in your mind that your catch has scored a bullseye. But he will still be interested in your story if the catch is a near-miss!

• *The Secretary of the British Record (rod-caught) Fish Committee is Mr Peter Tombleson, National Anglers' Council, 11, Cowgate, Peterborough, PE1 1LZ, telephone (day) Peterborough (0733) 54084 or evenings 252428.*

JOHN INGHAM

WORLD CHAMPS!

Teams of crack matchmen from 20 European countries meet once a year in the World Coarse Fishing Championships. Nations with facilities for staging this remarkable angling spectacular take turns at playing host. England has never won the world team title but in the separate individual championships our men have won the crown on four occasions, including the 1981 championships which came to England on the Warwickshire Avon at Luddington.

Above: Dave Thomas, a Leeds postal officer, became England's fourth individual world champion in 1981. Our picture shows Dave surrounded by admiring fans as he displays the two chub which helped his total weight of 1,190 grammes (appr. 2 lb. 11 oz.) to beat the best from 19 other countries at a venue swept by gales and swollen by heavy rain.

Left: Jackie Morziers, of the French team, tackles up for the start of the World Team Championships. In the foreground is Jackie's supply of bait for the match, including close on a gallon of minute bloodworms stored in a polystyrene container.

PICTURES: ANGLER'S MAIL LIBRARY

BEACH ACTION

Sea fishing is expanding more rapidly than any other branch of the sport, according to the latest official survey which assesses followers of sea and coarse fishing as virtually level in the numbers game. The chief reasons for this big swing to the sea undoubtedly include freedom of access compared with many hard-pressed inland venues plus the satisfying reward of sharing the catch at the family's supper table.

PICTURES: DAVE PLUMMER AND ANGLER'S MAIL LIBRARY

Above left: The cast: The rod reaches full compression as a beachcaster punches his lead seawards during a cod-hunting session near Spurn Point, Humberside.

Right: The strike: A fish has taken the bait and the angler reels in for what beach fans say is the most exciting moment . . . finding out what's on the end of the line!

Above right: The wait: Baits are anchored and now it's a matter of waiting for the fish to show interest. Rods are set high as a lone angler waits for the signal that his family's supper is just a strike away. But the wait could be in vain, for sea anglers suffer just as many disappointments as their freshwater colleagues.

Right: The prize: Winter cod fishing is a cold sport but frozen fishing fingers are soon forgotten in the exciting awareness that the cod have moved inshore in their search for food.

Anglers have a lot to learn from birds and animals in the competition for fish. But what is sport for one is food and survival for the other.

Left: A kingfisher is one of the most beautiful birds on the wing as it hunts near water. They are partial to sticklebacks, small gudgeon and stone loach. But did you know their bright colouring is a warning to other predators that a kingfisher's flesh is foul-tasting?

Top right: The heron is a specimen hunter supreme, operating in much the same way as its human counterpart, stalking alone in search of the quarry and relying on stealth. Herons live on small fish, grass snakes, frogs and rats.

Below: Seals are cumbersome on land but masters of the seas where they feed on squid, cuttlefish, salmon and trout.

THE OTHER ANGLERS

YOUNG EXPERTS

Angling will never be short of recruits. Thousands of expert youngsters graduate from the junior ranks every season as thousands more take their places on the nursery slopes. Today's young anglers are better equipped at comparably less cost and armed with more knowledge than any previous generation.

Above: Mark Blake, of Plymouth, shook local adults with this fine catch of three ling. Each fish tops 40 lb., with the biggest weighing a monster 45 lb.

Left: Jeremy Rickards is following in father's footsteps. He is the son of Barrie Rickards, the noted pike angler.Jeremy is pictured with a 6¾ lb. common carp hooked at a fishery near his Cambridgeshire home.

PICTURES: MIKE MILLMAN AND BARRIE RICKARDS

All-night queues are now a common sight at the annual opening of popular reservoirs stocked with trout. An annual guide to a wide range of these public fisheries is published in Angler's Mail every March and is now so comprehensive that a large slice of two consecutive weekly issues is required to cover them all.

Left centre: Matchman Roy Marlow, of Leicester, is one of thousands of coarse angling fans who like to cast a fly in the opening months of the season. Here he is poised to net a Rutland Water trout.

Right: All-rounder Dave Plummer, of Norwich, travelled to Avington fishery, near Winchester, Hampshire, to tackle this fine 4¼ lb. brook trout.

Above: The Hampshire Avon is one of Britain's finest trout and salmon rivers. These anglers are working a boat above Christchurch in the hope of intercepting a run of sea trout.

Top left: Two salmon anglers wait patiently for the king of the river to move into a deep pool on the River Teifi, Wales.

Bottom left: Pitsford, Northamptonshire, is one of many reservoirs now stocked with trout and open to all. This lone fly-fisherman is making the most of the last light at Pitsford.

PICTURES: PETER STONE, DAVE PLUMMER AND ANGLER'S MAIL LIBRARY

If you have never fished for pike on a cold winter's afternoon a beautiful sun-setting scene like this has passed you by. Steve Harper, of Norwich, who enjoys Nature's scenic effects all through the season, is silhouetted on the River Waveney, Norfolk, as he takes the strain of a specimen pike.

PICTURE: JOHN WATSON

10 MATCHFISHING TIPS

Knowing what to do and when to do it takes a lot of practise and experience when it comes to winning matches. KEN COLLINGS, skipper of the highly successful Dorking, Surrey, team, has gained extensive knowledge in 20 years on the Open match circuit. In this special feature he gives budding matchmen ten basic tips that may help gain a win or section placing.

Knowing what to do at the right time brings its rewards. Here is Ken Collings with his cheque and trophy earned by winning the Southern Top 20 League.

Bleak are money spinners!

MOST pleasure anglers dislike bleak as nuisance fish which snatch baits meant for bigger fish. But to a match angler bleak can be valuable make-weights and can even win matches. A couple of seasons ago I had just under 20 lb of them on a waggler to win a big gravel pit match.

Many reckon that bleak are easy to catch but the truth is they are the shyest, quickest and cleverest of all fish. So let's take a look at how to catch them.

Speed is all very well but it's more important to fish with a method that will catch bleak for the full five hours of a match. This is where the running line bleak rig comes into its own. In most instances, the bleak can be caught in great numbers close in but then they shy off and a pole is no good. When they start "going shy" a change to the running line will keep them coming.

With practise it is relatively easy to catch 100-plus fish an hour on running line. That adds up to 500 bleak in a normal length match and, in most cases, would be enough to win.

I prefer a lightweight 10 ft. long rod with a soft action tip so that I can pull into the fish rather than strike. It also helps to build up a rhythm for catching. "Snatching" at fish means you are in trouble.

Another reason for the soft tip is the terminal tackle. I attach the float bottom-end only using 1.7 lb main line to 8 and 12 oz hooklengths and a small fine-wire short-shank hook with the barb flattened.

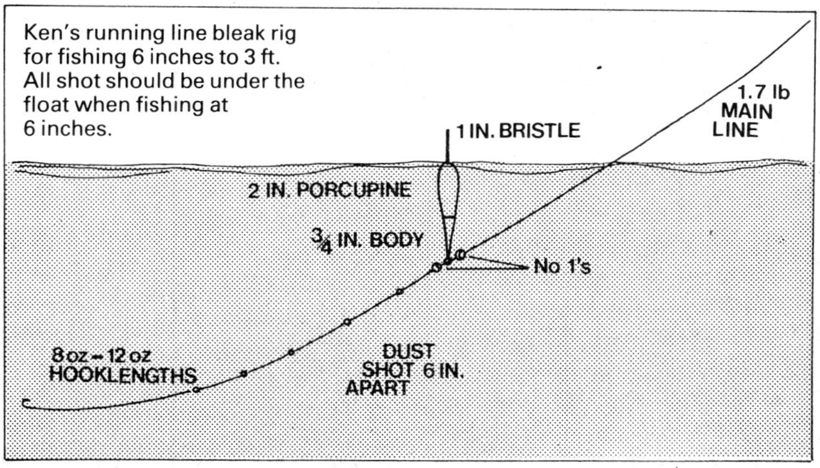

Groundbaiting to win

GROUNDBAITING is one of the most important factors in fishing but one of the least talked about. Basically, there are two types of groundbait, an ordinary white bread crumb from tackle shops and a brown non-sticky type known as Hovis. Both should be put through a "pinkie" sieve, which has one-sixteenth inch diameter holes, before being mixed with water.

How to mix groundbait depends on how the fish are feeding, the distance you are fishing at and how fast the water is flowing. But always remember that once you put in that first ball you must continue with the bait or put in enough to hold the fish from the start.

Add the groundbait to water, as this gives the best mix. It is difficult to give more detailed advice on groundbait in this limited space—all I can suggest is that you experiment during pleasure fishing trips or practise by throwing pieces of wood or stones in your garden so that your aim is good when you throw the actual groundbait from the riverbank.

Try out some additives, such as those used in the Continental groundbaits. Many of these are winners, as the French have proved in the World Championships. But we have a long way to go to catch up with what they know!

Switching hook sizes

WHEN struggling for bites go straight down to ultra-light gear. Don't bother changing down one hook size at a time. Go straight down from a No. 20 to a No. 26 and then change up one size at a time if you get a response and can keep getting bites.

You can also vary how much you are feeding, or try a different bait, but the light tackle approach will usually work if these two fail. Bear in mind that scaling down the hook also means putting either a "pinkie" or small home-bred maggot on the hook.

In the net as another roach falls for correctly-presented maggots.

The best way to beat fish on this light tackle is not to let them know they are hooked—just keep in touch with them. Obviously, you cannot really bend the rod into the fish, so just let it swim around tiring itself out and keep the line tight. Eventually, you will be able to get the fish swimming your way and into the landing net.

Get 'em on the drop

EVER fished in hot weather and failed to catch? Here's a way to get those shy fish—on the drop! This is allowing your bait to drop through the water so that it appears not to be on a hook or line.

There are two ways of doing this. Do not use any shot on the line or use No. 8's evenly spaced about 12 inches apart. You will probably get lift bites or the float will not settle properly but as soon as there is any indication you must strike.

A lot of bites will be missed, sometimes as many as 20 in a row but you will be getting bites and that means your chances of catching are high.

Casters or maggots on a fine wire No 18 hook, fished at anything from 9 inches to 3 feet, usually score. If there are any "skimmers" about try putting in a continuous cloud of groundbait.

Remember that the rig must be as light as possible, so don't use a weighted float. Try a piece of peacock quill about six to eight inches long with an insert and shot it well down, fishing with the line through the bottom end of the float only.

Home-bred maggots

ALL it takes to win some matches is an extra fish or two when fellow competitors are struggling for bites. I've found the best way to get these fish is to have a bait which is that bit different—a "special" or home-bred maggot.

The way I produce these is easy, cheap and has the advantage of giving clean maggots without any smell. All you need to start with is a piece of chicken, preferably breast, which will cost under £1 and give more than a quarter of a pint of maggots, which is more than enough for hook bait.

Buy the meat on a Friday and place it on some fresh bran in a bait box without any lid. Leave this outside to dry off in the fresh air. By Saturday it should have gone dry and, with any luck, there should be some fly blows on it. These are white and about the size of your small fingernail.

Around two or three blows are enough but don't worry if you have a few more. When you have the blows put the lid on the box and keep it where the temperature is not too hot or too cold.

Within five days the maggots should have eaten all the meat without any waste or smell. The hotter it is the faster the meat will go.

When the maggots come off the meat, around the next Friday, sieve them off into fresh, damp bran and you are ready to go fishing.

Win with swimfeeders

SWIMFEEDERS have created controversy on the Open match circuit over the past few years but I believe that fished correctly this is a skilful method and a match winner.

My conventional running water rig for a peg around 6 ft deep will consist of 4 lb reel line with a 1.7 lb hooklength and a feeder link. This is good for chub but the hooklength should be kept short and the feeder fished on a link of say, just three inches.

I use big maggots in the feeder and make sure they emerge quickly. It's no good reeling-in to find the bait still inside. Cut the holes and make them bigger if the water is slower as the faster the bait gets out the more use it is to you.

Don't be afraid to put more lead on the feeder to make it hold bottom. When fishing, always start at the top of the swim and try to pull the fish to your bait. If you start at the bottom of the swim you may scare them from your patch and then have nowhere left to fish for them.

It usually takes around 45 minutes to build up a swim and that's when to start searching around with the feeder.

I use a quivertip on running waters, which is just strong enough to hold the current, but prefer a springtip on stillwaters.

Winter weights

AS WINTER approaches, and water temperatures drop, the bags of small fish which had such a significant bearing on match results in the summer months become harder to put together.

No longer can you go to a match armed with only a tin of maggots and a bag of groundbait and expect to get a bite-a-cast everywhere you go.

It took me years to adapt and accept that methods which won more cash in the warm weather just won't work in colder months. This is the time of year when matches can be won or lost with one or two larger fish, such as barbel or chub. It is no coincidence that some anglers are continually coming up with these bonus fish.

Most times it's a case of putting yourself in for a win. You must set yourself a target weight. So do your

Who says swans and anglers don't get on? This swan took a liking to Ken's bronze maggots on a Thames fishing trip and wouldn't go away!

Get level with the water for good float control. Ken is able to descend from a high bank thanks to his waders but just in front of him the river drops away to 10 ft, so he has to be careful.

homework and find what weight you will need to make the frame. If you then find your catch rate is not good enough to reach the target it's time to make the frame. If you then find your catch rate is not good enough to reach the target it's time to switch to big fish.

Incidentally, when a swim suddenly "dies", this is a sure sign the big fish have moved in.

Baits? Casters are always a real "killer" for big fish. Those who always fish with casters come up with bonus chub and big roach. But don't neglect big baits. Big baits for big fish is how the saying goes and it's true.

My choice of hooks

HOOK selection seems to give trouble to many anglers. Hundreds have asked me what patterns I use. I always keep trying new ideas but here is a rough guide to some I have found to be good.

For general floatfishing with maggots I use a fine wire gold Mustad 204A, mainly in 18s and 20s. For casters, I prefer a long-shank blued model, Mustad 90204 in sizes 16, 18 and 20.

When legering in still or moving water I need a stronger hook and use a flat-forged reversed gold hook Mustad 39854 in 22s to 10s.

For pole fishing and bloodworms I use a long shank very fine wire barbless, Lion D'or 1219B in 20 to 26 sizes.

These are only an approximate guide as I use dozens of different hooks during a season and for different styles but it may give you a basis for experimentation and for finding the hook you prefer.

Set a new trend

BE trendy and win matches. I'm not talking about your fishing clothes but in all branches of angling, especially in match fishing, certain methods are successful for long periods.

For example, stick float and caster ruled for many years on the Trent. Then came the waggler and after that the bronze maggot.

Every venue has a current style which works time and time again. Knowing these methods and perfecting them are the first priorities of a good day's fishing.

The expected methods win more times than not, but if you are not catching fish, or want to lessen the odds, try something different.

Look at the success of the Nottingham anglers who travelled to the Welland, Thames and Nene and still scored with their own bronze maggots and wagglers.

Somebody had to start using maggots and wagglers on the Trent. Somebody had to use the feeder on the Severn.

So why not set the trend in your own area? Try something different and be successful.

Do it right and a net of fish like this can easily be yours in a match.

Pole-fishing basics

IT would take the whole of this Annual to tell you everything about pole fishing but for those just starting out I have drawn up a list of these basics:

- Start with a cheap pole of about 12 to 14 ft in three or four take-apart sections.
- Don't worry about all of the different attachments you can buy for the end. Just whip on an end ring.
- Make up winders with complete floats, hooks and lead before leaving home. You can then attach them to your pole on the riverbank.
- Shot floats at home in a milk bottle. Olivettes can be expensive so bulk your shot together.
- Use the right length of line fo r the pole length so you can swing small fish to hand. Allow for the bend in the pole with the weight of the fish.
- Do not strike. Just lift the pole upwards.
- Elastic can be used if catching big fish but without some practice you will just bounce out of fish.
- Plumb the depth accurately. Unless fishing "on the drop" I fish at the exact depth of the swim.

Ken Collings was talking to COLIN MITCHELL.

How a schoolgirl took on the lads at their own game

BIRMINGHAM teenager Claire Legge, the youngest ever to win the NFA Ladies National Championship title, talks to Beverly Adams about her angling career.

CLAIRE LEGGE had been fishing for only six years when she won the 1981 NFA Ladies National Championship title at 16 and became the youngest girl ever to do so.

Her remarkable career as a Birmingham match angler began in 1975 when she was only ten years old.

Claire takes up the story: "As a family we went fishing on the Warwickshire Avon and I watched my father, who had then recently taken up fishing again. He used to fish as a boy but gave it up for a while.

"I borrowed Dad's gear and had a go and when I caught my first fish I just wanted to carry on fishing. That's how it all started."

A few months later Claire entered her first fishing match—a preliminary round of a junior match. She qualified for the final with 9 oz but failed in the final.

CHAMPION CLAIRE!

"I won a prize, though, which kept me interested in matches," she recalls.

Her next event was the Birmingham AA Junior Championships in August 1976 where, again, she won a prize.

"I didn't catch very much but I won a girl's prize," says Claire.

By this time she knew how to cast quite well and was beginning to get the hang of things but realised there was still a lot to learn.

So she joined the Starlets AS, in Birmingham, after hearing about them at a presentation evening.

She says: "I was the only girl in the club but I wanted to learn more about fishing. They held a lot of matches and somebody was always on hand to put me right."

In 1977 she entered a junior match again and came third with 10½ oz of roach—"I was beginning to cope on my own now and knew a bit more."

Later that year she was top girl in the Birmingham Junior Championships and soon after that entered for her first senior competition.

"It was one of my Dad's works matches on the River Severn. I was the only junior taking part and I came sixth overall with 1 lb 14 oz.

"In the next senior match, another of Dad's works matches, I won with 2 lb 2 oz. But Dad wasn't so pleased—he came second!"

In that competition the going was hard and not many anglers caught fish but Claire showed she was gaining in technique by landing a chub, her only fish.

At this point Claire was concentrating hard on match fishing but still enjoyed pleasure fishing.

A turning point came in 1978 when she joined the Birmingham junior squad and was then picked for the Junior National on the Leeds-Liverpool Canal.

"I was a bit nervous before the start

Jubilant Claire after winning the 1981 Ladies National at a Wiltshire gravel pit.

Claire receives the runners-up trophy on behalf of Birmingham AA Junior team from Barrie Welham of Leeda Tackle, sponsors of the 1979 Junior National.

of the match but once it started I was all right," Claire admits and proved that by taking 1 lb 4½ oz and coming sixth in her section.

When fishing in competitions Claire found she was often one of very few girls fishing, sometimes the only one. But it didn't put her off.

"Some of the lads were a bit surprised at times," she chuckles.

In 1979, now 14, Claire was chosen to skipper the Birmingham Junior National team, the first girl to be given that honour.

"I don't really have a lot to do but one important job is to make the draw at the National. The trouble is I'm not very good at it and usually draw the wrong peg!" she declares ruefully.

Claire didn't do so well that year when the Junior National was held on the Warwickshire Avon at Evesham but made up for it with some successes later.

First, she won the Redditch Kingfisher Junior Championships, beating more than 100 with three carp for 9 lb 1 oz.

Then she fished her first Ladies National and came third in her section on the River Severn with two barbel for 5 lb 5 oz. At that time she was the joint youngest girl ever to fish in the National.

In 1980 she led the Birmingham team to victory in the West Midland Regional match and also took the individual title with 5 lb 3½ oz.

Even when she failed to do well in the Ladies National and the Junior National in 1980 Claire never considered giving up.

"Fishing has its ups and downs like everything. Even top anglers got dry nets so I didn't worry," says Claire with true angling philosophy.

She had one more match success in 1980 with a win in the ladies' section of the BAA Senior Canal Match with 1 lb 12½ oz.

Six years of dedication and determination finally paid off in 1981 when Claire entered the Ladies National, held on a gravel pit in Wiltshire and won it.

"That was my best match win and Dad was really pleased for me," she says with justifiable pride.

Claire is now too old for junior matches but still intends to compete at senior level.

Claire Legge and her father, Brian, with her angling trophies.

KNOW YOUR SEA FISH

ALWYNE WHEELER, of the Natural History Museum, London, describes the eight most common sea fish dealing with colouring and where the species normally live and what they eat.

NEXT to the cod family, the flatfishes are probably the most important group of sea fish to the angler as well as the fishing industry. But while the cod-fishes form a closely related group, the flatfishes are divided into several distinct families, so that in British seas there are no fewer than four main types and many more worldwide.

Flatfishes are unique in the way one eye moves during larval development so that by the time the young fish is fully formed both eyes are on the same side of the head and the fish is equipped to lie on the seabed both eyes facing upwards.

In certain of the groups it is always the same eye which moves so that the members of that group always lie on the same side and this is one of the main identifying features for flatfishes of all kinds.

BRILL

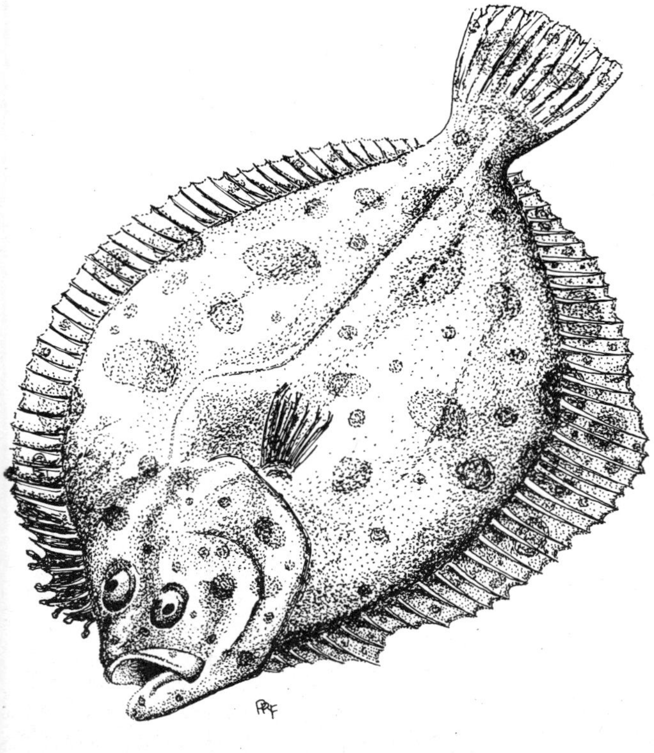

The brill is a member of the left-eyed flatfish family, in contrast to the plaice family which are right-eyed. Left-eyed flatfishes have both eyes on the left side of their head; thus they lie on their right side.

The brill's closest relations are the turbot, the megrims and the top-knots, which are really small and either deep-water species or very uncommon. These small species all have a distinguishing feature in that the dorsal and anal fins continue under the tail on the underside, not much in the megrims but with distinct lobes in the topknots. Neither the brill nor the turbot have such a continuation of these fins, they simply end on the sides of the tail.

Both turbot and brill are deep-bodied, broad fish with a moderately large head and big jaws. The two are hardly likely to be confused as the brill has small scales on the coloured side of the body and scales embedded in the skin on the white side. In contrast the turbot has bony tubercles giving the coloured side a rough appearance.

The brill's colouring is a dull sandy brown with small dark flecks and light spots on the left side, while the underside is creamy white. The fins are lighter in colour and the tail fin has no spots on it. In general the colouration of the "back" is an almost perfect match for the background on which the fish is lying.

Most of its food is comprised of bottom-living fishes, especially sandeels, whiting, pout and gobies. It also eats squid and large numbers of crustaceans, especially the brown shrimp and various crabs.

The brill spawns in late Spring and early summer and its eggs and newly hatched fry live close to the surface of the sea. During its development the fry drift inshore as a result of wind-driven sea currents.

At a length of about 1 inch it begins to live on the seabed and at this size, and a little bigger, the young fish can be caught in sandy-bottomed tide pools and in the breakers on the shore.

While these postage stamp-sized fish are of no interest to anglers they are strikingly beautiful miniatures of the big fish and although almost translucent they are a perfect match for their surroundings. As they grow, young brill move offshore and the adults are most common in depths of 30 to 200 feet of water on sandy bottoms, less often on gravel.

COALFISH

NO other fish has so many widely used names as the coalfish. Possibly the most common is saithe but locally, as on the north-east coast of England, it is known as billet.

In appearance, a coalfish is obviously a member of the cod family, although it almost always lacks the chin barbel characteristic of the family.

The characters it shares with the cod, and most other members of the family, are three dorsal fins and two anal fins, and the characteristic shape of the tail merging into the tail fin rays.

The presence of a chin barbel is often a matter of contention. In fact, when young (up to 3-4 inches) the coalfish does have a short barbel, but as it grows it becomes lost in the developing tissue on the chin.

The development of the lower jaw in large coalfish is quite striking, and the bone becomes massive. This also results in the lower jaw becoming longer than the upper as the fish grows, although they are equal length in young.

Too much is often made of the presence of absence of the chin barbel. Identification is much more certain from examination of the lateral line.

If there is still doubt about the identification of a fish the clinching detail comes in examining the gill rakers on the first gill arch.

Lift the gill cover and count the stiff light-coloured spiky rakers opposite the blood-red gills. If there are between 35 and 40, then the fish is a coalfish.

The coalfish is widely distributed in the North Atlantic, ranging from the English Channel northwards to the Arctic, around Iceland, the southern tip of Greenland and along the coasts of Canada and the northern states of the USA.

It forms large schools near the surface and in mid-water and in depths down to about 10 fathoms but it is common close inshore as well as in the open sea.

In northern waters, from Yorkshire northwards, the young fish are often abundant in a few feet of water among sea weeds and around rocks, and even in tidal pools.

These little fish are very beautifully coloured with dark green backs and upper sides and golden sides and creamy bellies. The adults are more dull, the green of the back giving way sharply to dull silver sides and belly. At all ages the lateral line is creamy coloured.

Up to two years of age, young coalfish are common in inshore waters and readily take bait. From observations made by archeologists, Neolithic inhabitants of the Inner Hebrides must have caught them by the thousand, for the shell middens of Oransay are full of coalfish bones.

COD

IT would not be difficult to make a case for the cod as the best-known sea fish in Britain. Not only is it a well-known food fish, caught commercially in large quantities by trawling, Danish seining, and on long lines, but it is an important angling fish.

Best known and present all year in northern waters, it is a familiar fish to Scottish anglers and those on the north-east of England, while elsewhere it becomes common in the winter.

There are few problems with cod identification. It has the typical cod family barbule on the tip of its chin and the characteristic structure of the tail fin with the body extending deep into the fin, flanked top and bottom with increasingly long fin rays.

The cod has three dorsal fins, all close together at the base, and rather round in outline. There are two anal fins which are closely set and the first of these has its origins beneath the second dorsal. The head is relatively large and the body fairly thick-set without spoiling the stream-lining of an active swimming fish.

Coloration is very variable although it always has a basic form which is standard. The back and upper sides are mottled, the lower sides and belly are creamy white, sometimes yellowish, but the clinching feature in colour characters is the white lateral line. It is always light in colour, no matter what shade the rest of the body.

The variability mostly concerns the colouring of the back and upper sides. Most cod caught on our coasts are dull green with yellowish mottling but some are very distinctly dull reddish with yellow mottling.

The variation is a response to the background colouring of its habitat. On sandy bottoms it is pale yellowish-green when living among seaweeds, and therefore reddish on rocky coasts. Young cod sometimes live among the sea-grass beds and they tend to be pronouncedly green in colouring.

Differences in colour are therefore

POUTING

If the coalfish qualifies for the title of the British sea fish with the most common names, then the pouting probably runs it a close second. Known variously as pout, pouting, bib or whiting-pout with the last name sometimes reversed to become pout-whiting, all are names for the same fish but their use often causes problems for a sea angler who knows the fish by one name and not the others.

Another potential source of confusion is that the coloration of the fish is variable with its habitat. A pouting caught over a sandy sea bed on the North Sea cost, where it is very common, will be a sandy-brown fish with silvery-white belly and a conspicuous black spot at the base of the pectoral fin.

But a pouting from a wreck on the south-west coast is a beautiful coppery-brown with yellowish sides and white belly, and the sides have five dusky cross-bands. The pectoral fin base has the same conspicuous black spot.

The development of the dusky cross bars seems to be due partly to size. They become more conspicuous as the fish grows older but is also on account of the clearer water and better visibility. Whatever causes the differences in colouring it sometimes makes one look hard at the fish just to check identification.

The pouting is a member of the codfish family and has many of the characters of the cod. The most obvious are the three dorsal fins and two anal fins, the bases of which actually overlap in the pouting, and the long chin barbel. The tail fin has the structure typical of the cod family.

The only fishes with which the pouting is likely to be confused are the smaller Poor Cod and Norway pout. The pouting is distinctly deeper-bodied than either of these. Its snout is prominent—the lower jaw is shorter than the upper—but the reverse is true of the Norway pout which also has a space between the second and third dorsal fin bases. In the pouting the first anal fin origin is beneath the middle of the dorsal fin but in the Poor Cod its origin is level with the beginning of the second dorsal fin. The Poor Cod also has only a small dark spot at the base of the pectoral fin, but it is very conspicuous in the pouting.

The long barbule and underside of the head have numerous taste organs on them and in the pouting the long rays of the pelvic fins are also well equipped. The pouting swims over the sea bed with these rays bent downwards and forwards and they clearly play an important role in finding food. It feeds very heavily on buried crustaceans, especially shrimps and amphipods, like the sandhopper, and clearly it locates these with either barbule or fins. It also eats some fishes and the wreck or reef-dwelling larger fishes are active predators on small fishes and squids.

usually associated with locality and experienced fishermen can often tell where a catch has been made by registering the coloration of the fish.

The cod is widespread in the North Atlantic . On our side of the ocean it ranges from Northern Biscay, where it is an uncommon, winter visitor, and northwards far up into the Arctic, and the coasts of northern Norway and the USSR.

It is abundant off Iceland and the southern tip of Greenland, then southwards off the Canadian coast and to the northern United States. A very closely-related species is found in the North Pacific.

Through this huge range it establishes a number of local races, but although these are important from the view-point of regulating the fishery in certain areas, they need not cause problems for the angler. In Europe the only very distinct local population is the Baltic cod which is sufficiently different from the other populations to be recognized as distinct sub-species. But it is confined to the Baltic so it will not cause identification problems to British anglers.

WHITING

THERE can be few sea anglers who have not caught or seen a whiting for it is one of the most common and widely-distributed of the members of the cod fish family in our seas.

Commercial fishermen also take considerable quantities of whiting particularly in the North and Irish Seas, while the western Scottish coast and the Bristol Channel also offer considerable fisheries. Due to its relatively small size, however, the catch of whiting in terms of weight never approaches the huge weights of cod or haddock landed an anglers or commercial fishermen.

The whiting is not a fish which gives any real problems in identification. Like other members of this branch of cod family it has three dorsal fins, two anal fins and the typical tapering tail leading into the characteristic tail fin.

But unlike its closest relatives it has no barbule on the tip of the chin. This distinguishes it from several relatives like the bib or pouting and the poor cod, while the spacing of the dorsal and anal fins, close together in the whiting, distinguishes it from saithe and pollack which have well-spaced dorsal and anal fins.

The only other fish which could possibly be confused with the whiting is the blue whiting or poutassou, sometimes called Couch's whiting, commemorating the man who first found it on the British coast.

The blue whiting has three dorsal and two anal fins and has no chin barbule but the dorsal fins are separated by wide spaces, not close together as they are in the whiting. In fact, confusion should never really occur as the blue whiting is a midwater fish living mainly in the open sea. Its back is blue and sides silvery white, but the back colour fades to slate grey soon after death.

Interestingly, within the last few years the blue whiting has become quite abundant in the western Channel, but usually well offshore, a result, it is thought, of changes in the major ocean currents of the Atlantic.

The ordinary whiting, however, is inconspicuously coloured, the back being sandy brown to greenish brown and the belly conspicuously white, silvery when alive. These modest tones fade quickly after death. The base of the pectoral fin has a conspicuous rounded dusky patch, and this is a useful feature in identification.

One reason why the whiting is so familiar is that it lives in shallow water inshore and is thus well within range of the beach angler as well as the smallest boats. Adult whiting are most common at depths of 60-250 ft and live close to and often on the bottom, mainly over sand, shell or gravel.

They feed on a wide range of fishes particularly bottom-living species like sandeels and gobies, but also prey on young herring, sprats and other members of the cod family which are caught in mid-water, not just on the seabed. Both young and adult whiting eat large numbers of brown shrimps and other small crustaceans and locally these can be their most important food.

For all its modest size and appearance the whiting has one particularly interesting aspect of behaviour. The young fish, at a length of about one to two inches, live with big jellyfishes following them around as they float in the sea surface currents and hiding among the tentacles which are armed with stings, lethal to most small fish. They manage to avoid getting stung themselves and presumably enjoy protection from larger predatory fish by this life style.

HADDOCK

HADDOCK are among several familiar fishes found on both sides of the North Atlantic, As with the cod, saithe, mackerel, and herring it is common to the coasts of Canada and the United States as well as to Europe.

All are members of the distinctive Boreal fauna (named from Boreas the Latin name for the north wind) which dominates most of the seas round Britain and provides many of the most valuable commercial fishes as well as angling species.

The haddock is a member of the cod family which is typical of this Boreal fauna, as its chin barbule, three dorsal fins, and two anal fins, and two anal fins go to show. It also has the distinctive junction of tail-to-tail fin of the cod fish family. Although it has several relatives in northern European waters, none are close relatives, and the haddock is thus well distinguished from all our other fishes.

One of the minor distinguishing points is its triangular first dorsal fin, which rises to a sharp apex, very dissimilar to that of most other cod fishes. This, however, is not an important feature.

When identifying, the most immediate distinguishing character is its colouring, especially the rounded sooty mark on the side above the pectoral fin and the black lateral line. The back is sandy to greeny-blue, the sides and belly conspicuously white but haddock caught in clear shallow water are often a beautiful coppery colour with golden sides.

Other features of importance for identification are the short lower jaw, and curved snout, so that the mouth is small and largely ventral, and the large eye.

The mouth situated totally on the underside of the head suggests that the haddock feeds mainly on the seabed. Examination of the stomach

POLLACK

THE Pollack's nearest relative is that fish of many names, the coalfish or saithe. The two are closely similar and clearly close relatives.

Yet, where the coalfish is widely distributed across both sides of the North Atlantic, the pollack is rather restricted in its range. It is essentially a European fish which ranges to the southern coast of Iceland and the north of Norway, southwards to southern Spain, and the Spanish, French and Italian coasts of the western Mediterranean.

At both the northern and southern extremities of its range, however, it is rare. As a result the Channel coast of France and the coasts of the British Isles are about the centre of its range, where it is both common and is caught in numbers.

Its close relationship with the coalfish means that identification problems arise when attempting to distinguish between the two species. Coloration is some help as the back is brownish, green shading to yellowish green on the sides, the underside being white. The lateral line, however is dark (it is always light in the coalfish).

The shape of the lateral line is also characteristic. In the pollack it has a sharp curve above the pectoral fin and then continues straight along the midline (compare this with the coalfish which is virtually straight from head to tail).

In small and half-grown pollack the lower jaw is distinctly more prominent than in coalfish of the same size, but in fish approaching 10 lb. in weight there is hardly any difference in the shape of the jaw in the two species.

When confirmation of identification is particularly important the absolute clinching features is the number of gill rakers on the first gill arch. These are counted by lifting the gill cover and counting the hard, light coloured spiky rakers that lie oposite the blood-red gill rays on the gill arch. Pollack usually have 26 or 27 gill rakers, compared with 35-40 in the coalfish. Unfortunately, the fish has to be killed to make an accurate count.

The pollack is very much an angler's fish, and is rarely caught by commercial fishermen. This is partly because its natural habitats are the rocky reefs, rough ground, and wrecks that are shunned by trawlermen.

It forms small schools when it is small but they become loose aggregations when the fish gets larger and the really large pollack often seem to be loners.

Young fish with their schooling instincts seem to be less confined to rocky habitats and occur on sandy bottoms and in estuaries. The depth-range of the pollack is from the surface down to about 100 fathoms.

Although a common fish the pollack's biology is little known. It seems to be a slow-growing species which, by its fifth year, reaches a length of about 20 inches which suggests that the really large pollack of 20 lb. may be as old as 20 years. If this is true (and it is only an estimate) then it is clear that heavy exploitation of the wrecks and reefs inhabited by these big fish will have serious consequences to the numbers of pollack over a long period.

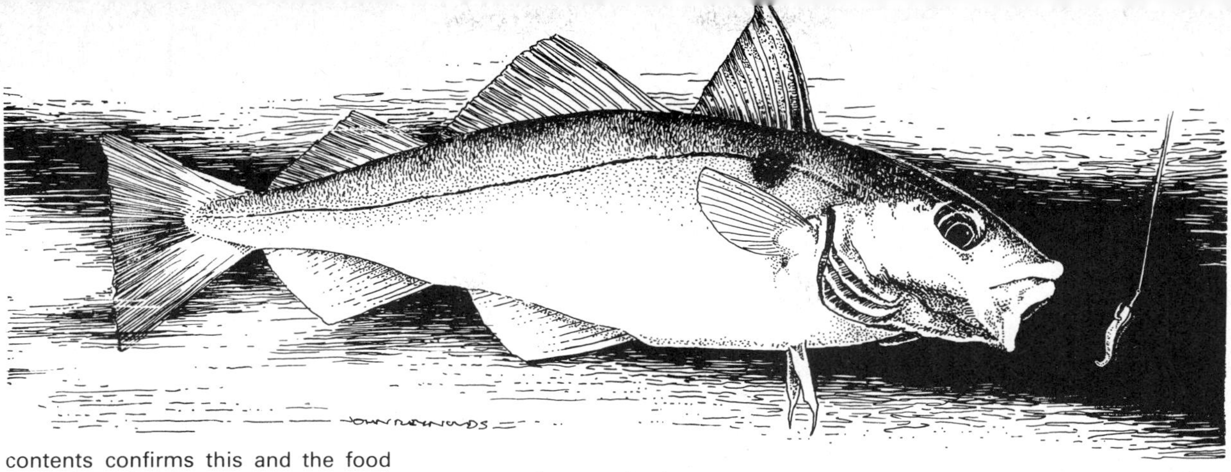

contents confirms this and the food comprises brittlestars, worms and molluscs.

Occasionally, but only in certain areas, haddock will eat quantities of sponge and this imparts to the gut and sometimes to the flesh of the fish a most offensive "chemical" smell. But the diet of haddock almost anywhere in their range includes something which makes them smell objectionable and gutting a large catch of haddock can be a very smelly operation!

The great majority of haddock live in rather deep water, from 20 150 fathoms, but they do occur in numbers in shallower water than this. Generally speaking it is mainly young fish in their second or third year and thus between 12 and 18 inches long that are found in shallow water, but occasionally a much bigger specimen will be caught.

Haddock spawn mainly in Spring and the eggs float at the surface, as do the post-larvae and fry. Haddock fry, however, have the fascinating habit of swimming alongside and underneath jellyfishes. They seem to avoid being stung by jellyfish tentacles but it is not certain what advantage they find in living so close to a potential predator although they probably gain some protection from other predators.

LING

LING belong to a branch of the cod family that includes the rocklings and the burbot. In this group the chin barbule is well developed and there are two dorsal fins, the first short-based and the second long.

They also have a single long-based anal fin which contrasts with the true cod fishes which have three dorsal fins and two anal fins. The ling and its relatives are also slender-bodied, in fact the ling is almost eel-like in body shape.

These features are generally all that are necessary to identify a ling caught by angling round the British coast.

Coloration is very variable and depends on the habitat, especially the depth, at which the fish was caught. The back is mottled; dull browny green, but lighter below, and there is a dark patch at the rear edge of the first dorsal fin and fainter blotches on the second dorsal and anal fins. The edges of these fins are light.

Trawlers on the west coast catch two other kinds of ling—the blue ling, a species ranging from Norway and Iceland southwards to the northern coast of Ireland and the Spanish ling, which as its name suggests, occurs to the south in the Mediterranean, off Spain, Portugal, and northwards to the Scottish coast.

Both are deep-water fishes rarely found shallower than 200 fathoms, and neither grows as large as the ordinary ling. Neither has been caught by anglers, although their capture is just possible on the west coast of Ireland.

A useful distinguishing point for both is that the lower jaw protrudes beyond the upper (the opposite is true of the ling), both have rather long pelvic fins, and are more slender in the body than the ling.

The ling is mainly a deep-water fish, common at depths of 150 fathoms, but also found in much shallower water of 10-12 fathoms. Inshore it is most common on rocky grounds, close to reels, and it also inhabits wrecks. Its food is principally fishes, but scientific studies of its diet are few and rather unsatisfactory.

Pouting, cod, Norway pout, pollack and gurnard have been found in their stomachs and ling is also known to eat octopuses in some numbers.

One of the problems in assessing its diet is that being a deep-water fish its swimbladder explodes if it is brought to the surface normally and its stomach everts. Thus, it is often impossible to assess what a fish has eaten.

The ling spawns in deep water in Spring and early summer, and after a brief period at the surface the young fish lives on the seabed. In northern waters young ling of six to nine inches may be found in inshore shallows of 8-20 fathoms, but they are not often captured.

Growth is slow, and by the end of the third year they may only measure up to 22 inches in length. Males rarely live longer than 10 years, but the females continue to grow until they are 14 and more years of age. So most large ling are females and the biggest specimens are probably 20 or more years of age, an important point to bear in mind if the conservation of stocks is to be considered.

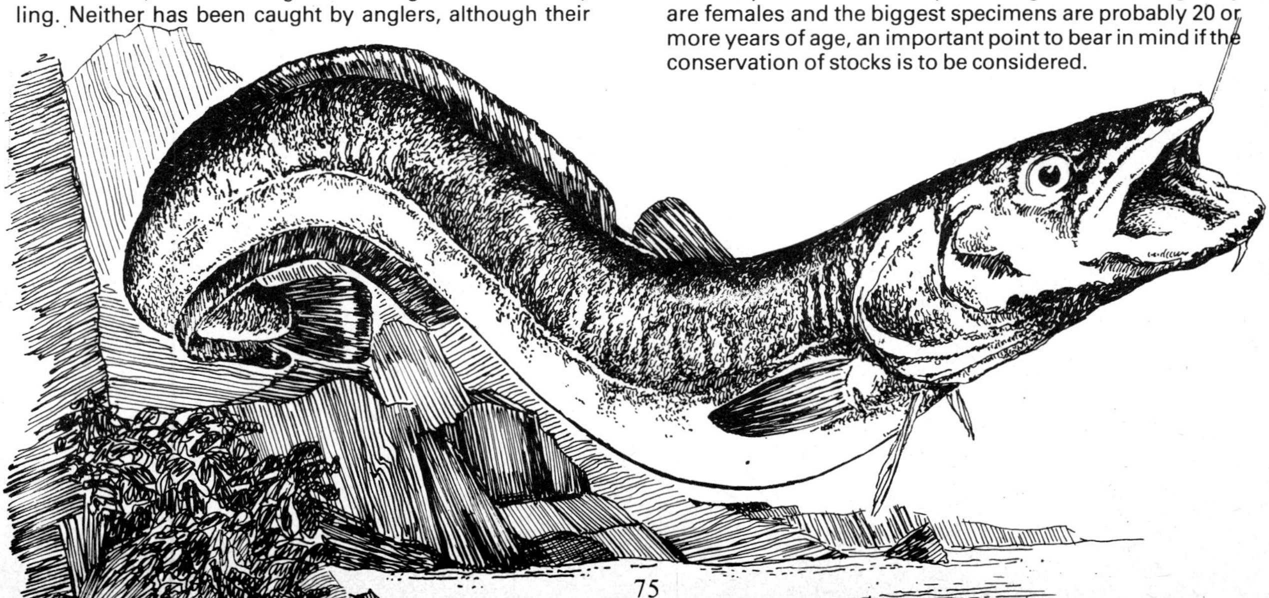

FISH KEEPING IS

YOU would probably be surprised to know just how many people find it relaxing and interesting to keep fish rather than to catch them. Not the same types of fish, of course, but the small, brightly-coloured species generally known as "tropicals".

Despite their exotic appearance, tropical fish are in many ways easier to keep, and certainly more interesting, than the traditional goldfish almost everyone has had at some time or another.

Their requirements are simple: a stable temperature, clean water, and correct feeding—in short, duplicating what would be found in their natural environment. Fortunately, most of those things can be provided automatically, thanks to modern technology, leaving the hobbyist free to concentrate on the more interesting aspects of fishkeeping.

A frameless aquarium, with lighting concealed in a flush-fitting cover, can be a pleasing addition to a lounge.

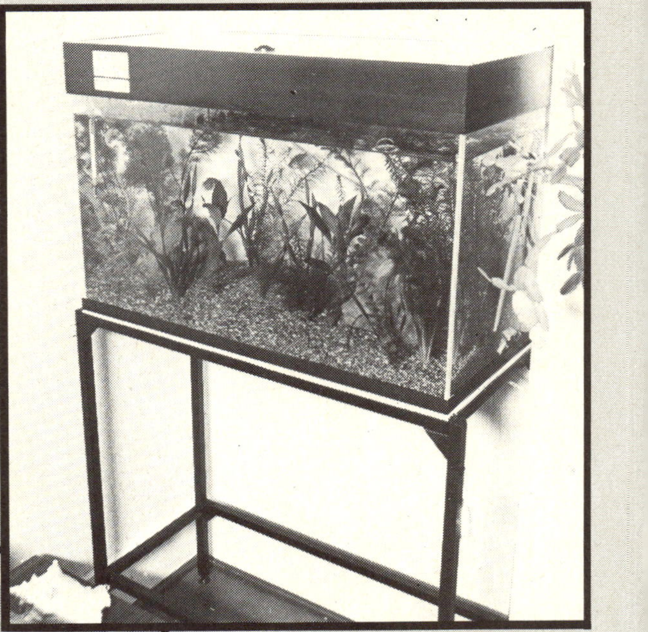

Below is how most people imagine tropical fish. Small, bright, almost translucent fish, swimming about in an illuminated tank.

Let's look first at the equipment needed. The aquarium will probably be made with silicone rubber, an incredibly tough adhesive that is used to stick together the sheets of glass into a frameless, watertight cube. An aquarium constructed in this way will never leak, nor is there any iron frame to rust, though you can get some tanks with a plastic or aluminium frame that is purely decorative.

The best size of aquarium for a beginner is between 24 in. and 36 in. long; anything smaller will prove more difficult to keep in a healthy state. Very large aquaria are expensive and may need special types of equipment.

You will also need somewhere to stand the aquarium. If there is a convenient shelf or cabinet make sure it will take the weight as a filled aquarium 24 in. long will weigh more than an adult. So don't take unnecessary chances! A suitable tubular-steel stand is obtainable from a local dealer if you are in any doubt. You will also need a cover to fit on top of the aquarium. This serves two purposes by reducing the rate of evaporation of the water and housing the lighting that is essential if plants are to grow well. Purchase a properly-designed cover from a dealer, or use a sheet of glass to cover the tank and make a box-like lighting unit to fit on top.

A thermostatically-controlled electric aquarium heater is needed to keep the water at the right temperature for the fish. This is encased in a metal or glass tube and must be kept immersed in the water whenever switched on. The fish will need a constant temperature of around 75°F, (which is about the level of a typical summer's day), and the heater will provide that automatically.

Finally, a filter must be fitted to help keep the water clean and pure for long periods, otherwise you will have to clean the aquarium completely every few weeks like a goldfish bowl. The simplest filters are worked from an air pump, passing the water through a layer of special nylon wool that traps the unsightly waste matter in the aquarium. Another type of filter consists of a flat plate which is placed beneath the gravel and is known as a biological filter. The most expensive filters are motorised, called "power filters", and these are particularly suitable for large aquaria.

SETTING UP

Wash out the aquarium carefully in clean, warm water to remove dust, fingermarks and so on. Be careful, because a wet tank is a very slippery object. Check that the stand or shelf to be used is absolutely level, using a spirit level, then cut 1 in. wide strips of expanded polystyrene to pad all round the outer edge of the aquarium where it is in contact with the stand. This ensures that any slight unevenness in the surfaces will not damage the tank.

Next wash the gravel under cold water, a little at a time in a clean bucket, and tip it gently into the tank: you will need about 14lb of gravel for each square foot of base area. Then fill the aquarium two-thirds full with cold water straight from the tap and add whatever decorative rocks or slate you

FUN!

· by Cliff Harrison

have selected after washing them like the gravel.

At this stage the water will probably be looking pretty murky but don't worry, it will clear within a few days.

Now instal all the equipment—heater, lighting and filtration in accordance with the manufacturers' instructions and check that everything is working correctly: if it is, you can leave the aquarium for a few days before adding the plants and fish.

In a tropical aquarium, the plants really will grow provided you give them the correct lighting. One 40 watt bulb per square foot of surface area, for about 12-14 hours per day, should be about right: don't put the aquarium too near a window, because you have little control over sunlight.

Choose some of the fast-growing, background plants like Ambulia, Myriophylum, Hygrophila and Vallisneria, together with a few of the more interesting varieties like Cryptocorynes, Aponogetons, Echinodorus and Amazon Swords.

A modern 'cube-style' tank sited on a brick plinth can make a very attractive feature point.

A leopard catfish is a popular inmate for tropical tanks.

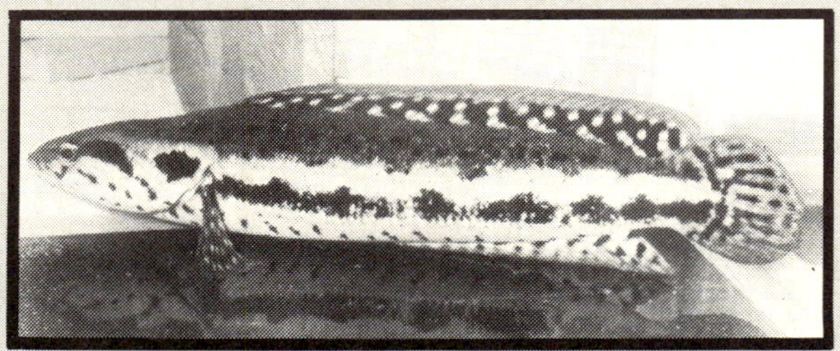

Not all tropical fish are small and timid—The "snakehead" can grow up to 30 inches long and give a nasty bite with its teeth!

THE COST

These are typical costs of setting up an aquarium measuring 24 inches long, 12 inches wide and 15 inches high:

It is possible to spend far more than this on a tank; models are available that come complete in wooden cabinets to form attractive pieces of furniture, others are wall-mounted to save floor space. A local dealer will advise on the different types.

Tank	from £9.00
Lighting	from £6.00
Heating	£8.50
Aeration/Filtration	from £5.50
Gravel/Rocks	£2.50
Plants	£2.00
Fish	from 30p each
Stand (if needed)	£15.00

When you purchase the fish, the dealer will place them in a sealed plastic bag. They will live like this for a couple of hours or more but don't let them get chilled. When you get home float the bag in the aquarium for about 15 minutes to equalise the temperatures, then carefully cut open the top of the bag and let the fish swim out.

Those you choose will depend on personal taste but ensure they will live happily together. Interesting, inexpensive community-tank fish include Neons, Cardinals, Zebras, Glowlights, Harlequins, Checker Barbs, Platies, Kuhli Eels, Pearl Gouramies and Lemon Tetras. On the other hand, you may prefer some of the more specialist fish, like Angels, Siamese Fighters or Catfish. The dealer will advise on the species which can be kept together.

There is so much more to fishkeeping than just watching a tank full of pretty creatures. There is the challenge of breeding the more unusual types, and eventually you may decide to try your hand with tropical marine fish, such as the beautiful Clowns and Butterflies.

There are hundreds of different species to choose from, some reaching to two feet or more in length, others like the Piranha and Electric Catfish, are positively dangerous! Whoever said fishkeeping was a dull pastime?

Preparing for a long-stay fishing

WEEK-ENDERS START HERE!

BY JOHN BAKER

The rewards of a long session as author John Baker displays fine mirror and common carp.

As each new coarse fishing season begins, the long days and warm summer nights attract carp anglers who are prepared to spend whole weekends, or even a week's holiday beside a favourite water in the hope of a good catch.

When preparing for one of those long sessions a little thought and planning will help to make your stay comfortable and successful.

I have always enjoyed preparing for a weekend of carping and look on this as half the fun. There is an air of expectancy as I pack away the tackle carefully and prepare the bait, checking and rechecking every item to ensure a successful session.

Over the years I have adopted a routine of preparation which rarely lets me down. There was even a time when I typed out a check-list to make sure I would not forget a thing!

CHOICE

Tackle and bait are obviously the most important and the choice depends entirely on the venue chosen. It is pointless taking all the tackle you possess as you may well spend more time carrying it from swim to swim than actually fishing with it.

Try to find out as much about the water as possible before the visit and plan accordingly. If the water is open and relatively weed free, then light tackle is all that is required. If some long-range fishing is expected check that spools are filled to the maximum and that you have plenty of heavy leads. Simple things but so important on the day.

Spending a couple of days at a water is a great opportunity to look for the fish, which are bound to show themselves by leaping and rolling, bubbling, or colouring the water by bottom activity.

Don't be content to sit behind a couple of rods waiting for the carp to come to you. Arm yourself with a pair of Polaroids, which will cut out some of the surface glare on the water, and wander carefully around the lake with "roving" tackle, including rod, landing net and bait.

Inspect the weedbeds and margins for basking or feeding fish, peer under overhanging bushes or tree branches along the bankside. On the right day you could be pleasantly surprised.

SESSIONS

Choice of bait is an individual matter but for long sessions there are only a few points to watch. Always take a bait in which you have confidence, preferably one which has been successful in the past. By all means experiment but don't rely on a new, untried bait.

Particle or multiple baits are best kept in the liquid in which they were cooked. This may smell after a few days but the carp are not put off and seem to prefer it.

Be prepared to take a little more bait than normally required for a day trip. A gallon of seeds or beans is not too much for a two or three-day session. The same applies to paste or boiled baits. A little more time spent making up extra amounts is often worth the effort, even if it takes a long time. What could be worse than to run out of bait when the carp are really feeding? About two pounds of made-up paste or 250-300 boiled baits is ideal for a weekend session.

On arriving at the water a good routine to follow is to try to find the fish first, depending on swim availability and time of day. Wherever you decide to "set up" catapult a few baits into the likely area and watch events. Try to "hold" the fish in the area rather than draw them to you.

If no bites are forthcoming do not catapult more bait but wait and watch for signs of carp or go and search for them. Heavy prebaiting is effective but only if you are positive the carp are feeding confidently or are likely to feed in your swim.

SAMPLES

Surprisingly enough, carp seem to have very little difficultly in finding one single bait laying on the lake bed even if no free samples surround it.

All waters vary, so if banking on one bumper session at a venue you have not fished before it may pay to spend several hours talking to other anglers and getting the feel of the water before starting to fish.

Bait freshness is not a worry on a long session. I am quite happy using baits which are several days old providing they are firm and not mildewed. Paste baits tend to "go-off" more quickly then boiled baits and for this reason I prefer to boil my baits when on a long stay. The alternative is to take ingredients and make baits up on the bank. This is a good idea but time consuming and rather fiddly.

Long days and nights beside a lake or riverbank away from the comforts of home can be difficult to endure. Plenty of food and drink is essential as these help to make the stay more tolerable.

Many carp anglers are tea addicts, each equipped with a favourite old kettle. It is not uncommon for them to brew-up every hour on the hour! A well stocked food bag is a must for any fishing trip, but contents should vary according to the weather.

Milk, cheese, butter or fresh meats may go off in a heatwave, so avoid taking these and substitute with dried milk, margarine, dehydrated food, biscuits and plenty of soft drinks.

I like to take snacks such as peanuts, shortbreads, cheese-biscuits, apples and so on. A small camping gas cooker is ideal for making soft drinks.

SOUPS

Most shops sell ready-made soups and other meals which may be prepared in a few minutes with hot water in a cup. Alternatively a tin of stew can be heated quickly in a small pan. Most tins of stew contain potatoes and vegetables as well as meat, so it is a meal-in-one.

The last, but most vital thing we must look at before setting out, is that we are properly clothed and have the other essentials vital for a long session beside a water.

One of the most popular pieces of equipment used by carp anglers today is the bed-chair or sun-lounger. Light, strong and ideal for a comfortable night's sleep they convert easily to an upright fishing chair.

The usual drill is to fold up a

No self-respecting long session angler would be without his faithful old kettle. Apart from bait this is probably the most important item of gear!

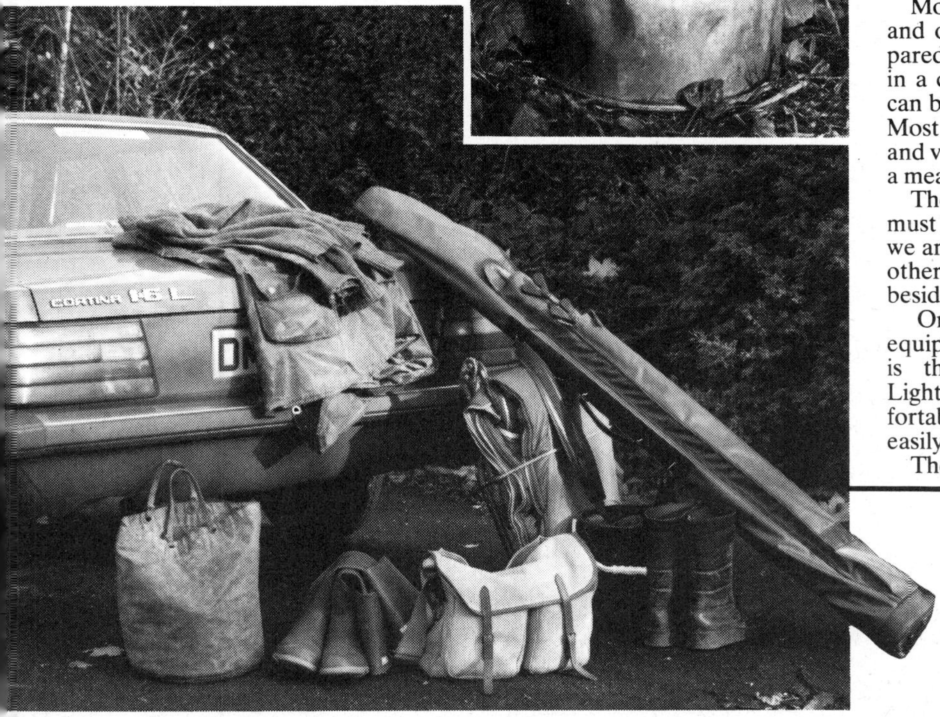

Ready to start. All the gear has been checked off the packing list and is now ready for loading in John Baker's car.

All set up and now the long wait starts. Taking the right kit means the session stands a good chance of being pleasant and successful.

John Baker plays an early-season fish caught during a long session at a Cambridgeshire gravel pit.

sleeping bag, groundsheet and blanket in the chair and keep it all in place for carrying with a hook-end car elastic. The whole package should weigh no more than about 16 lb.

A large 45-inch umbrella is adequate for keeping angler and tackle dry. Some prefer the added comfort of a Brolly-tent, but this may restrict your fishing and force you to "set-up" too far away from the rods.

FOOTWEAR

Waders are useful but can become uncomfortable in hot weather or for a long period, so it is worth taking a light pair of boots or shoes to wear when waders are not required.

A waterproof jacket, preferably with lots of pockets, is useful for carrying bits and pieces, especially when stalking fish. Alternatively a light over-jacket is ideal for wet weather.

Jumpers and trousers should be drab in colour. Army surplus stores supply a good and cheap selection of this type of clothing.

A spare pullover and spare socks are always worth taking. All other essentials are mentioned in my check list and by cutting down on items which are heavy, or take up a lot of space, its surprising how little is actually required for a weekend's fishing.

JOHN'S CHECK LIST

Rods ● Reels & spools ● Rod rests & buzzers ● Brolly or brolly-camp ● Landing net pole ● Hooks, weights, floats ● Swivels, beads, oddments ● Catapults ● Indicators/isotopes ● Sacks ● Weigh-bag ● Scales ● Spare line ● Forceps ● Sharpening stone ● Tea, coffee ● Sugar ● Milk (dried) ● Cup, plate ● Cutlery & tin opener ● Saucepan, kettle ● Frying pan ● Water ● Butter, fat ● General food ● Bread ● Sweets, snacks ● Soft drinks ● Gas stove ● Matches ● Groundsheet ● Sleeping bag, blanket ● Old towel, tissues ● Waders, boots ● Hat & spare socks ● Jumpers & jacket ● One-piece suit ● Alarm clock & torch ● Polaroid sunglasses ● Camera quipment & film ● Licences & Keys ● Bottom baits, floaters ● Particles, floaters ● Bed-chair, other chair ● Money & toothbrush!

Waterside Wildlife

Breakfast! Another small fish ends as a quick snack for an otter. But only a relative few are now left compared with their widespread distribution 200 years ago, says wildlife writer Michael Leach.

Angling is a superb pastime for millions of enthusiasts who enjoy the tranquility of a quiet river. But for most people that is all there is to it . . . a hobby, a delightful way of spending leisure hours.

It is so easy to forget that all the time we are by the waterside we are surrounded by animals which need to catch fish in order to survive. They are the other fishermen.

One of the most beautiful sights to be seen by any river is a hunting kingfisher. These silent birds are one of nature's best fishermen and have evolved a technique similar to their human counterpart.

A kingfisher will sit patiently on a twig overhanging the water and wait until a suitable meal swims past. They are very partial to sticklebacks and small gudgeon,

The Other Fishermen

with an occasional stoneloach for variety.

Moving with incredible speed that registers as only a blue blur, a kingfisher dives into the water and comes up carrying a fish. Normally, they take fish small enough to be swallowed whole and always head first to prevent the scales sticking in their throats and choking them.

Animal fishermen are solitary individuals. Like some humans they hunt alone as this makes the catching easier. The master of the secretive approach is the grey heron, which will not tolerate even the presence of another heron on a fishing expedition.

STEALTH

Herons rely on stealth, which is surprising considering their size, around three foot tall. They stand for hours in shallow water, or walk so slowly it is difficult to see they are moving at all.

Their long, agile necks are curved into an "S" shape, coiled like a spring. When a fish is spotted the spring is effectively released and the head catapults forward. Large species, such as pike, are speared with a razor-sharp four-inch beak.

Herons enjoy a comprehensive diet. As well as bullhead, stickleback and perch, they will also eat grass snakes, frogs and rats. There are only 4,000 pairs in Britain but herons appear to be everywhere because they have huge territories and will often fly more than 10 miles to find a suitable marsh or river in which to feed.

Shags and cormorants are a familiar sight around the coast, and sometimes in estuaries and inland lakes. They have learned to accept man and can live happily on a wide variety of fish. These birds are numerous and, except for the ever-present threat of a massive oil slick, will probably always be with us. Both use the same methods of finding a meal by diving a depth of around 30 feet and swimming under water, catching as they go.

by MICHAEL LEACH

Cormorants are so talented at fishing that for centuries the Japanese used them on a commercial basis. A band of leather or metal was fixed around the bird's neck and the cormorant was released. After diving and coming up with a fish, the bird was unable to swallow it because the neck band was too tight. A long cord connected the cormorant to a man standing on the shore and as soon as the bird was seen to be carrying a fish it was hauled in and relieved of the catch for the process to begin again.

By modern standards half of the cormorant's diet is unmarketable as few people eat coal fish and sand eels. But these are relatively recent aversions for early anglers ate almost anything that was brought in.

Another striking coastal fishing bird is the puffin, a stumpy little character with an outrageously coloured beak that is particularly noticeable in the breeding season.

Puffins spend many months living and hunting in the open sea, coming to land only to rear their young. The chicks thrive on a diet of sand eels and pollack.

EMOTIONS

But not only birds make their living in our waters. There are also a handful of mammals, including seals which arouse mixed emotions in anglers.

In the Orkneys, professional fishermen welcome the appearance of grey seals as they prey on squid and cuttlefish, keeping them away from the lobster pots.

But among others there are two schools of thought. One maintains it is a waste of time trying to catch anything in an area where a seal has been seen, as all the fish will have been frightened off. The counter-argument says the seal may have found a good run of fish and the catching rate should be high.

We have two resident species of seals, the grey and the common, and often it is not easy to tell them apart. The grey seal is bigger and has a very pointed head. Unfortunately, these animals take salmon and trout, which makes them less than popular with the crews of fishing boats. But they do eat a lot of sea creatures we don't want, such as octopus and squid.

INTELLIGENCE

Otters are the most attractive of all the wild "fishermen" and their high intelligence and sense of play have earned them a special place in the British countryside.

But, sadly, they are disappearing at an alarming rate and have now become a very endangered animal. They could be found throughout Europe 200 years ago, but this has changed and the stronghold of the otter is now in Scotland, where they are left in peace to live and breed. In the whole of England and Wales there may now be less than 100.

Early otter hunting was justified by the fact that they took a large number of game fish. But detailed research has proved that 90 per cent of their food consists of coarse fish and they are specially fond of eels.

Otter hunting is now illegal, but they are still perilously close to extinction. They have to be allowed to recoup their numbers if there is to be any chance of saving them. They require clean, unpolluted rivers and no disturbance which, after all, is exactly what the rest of us want. It is a rare occurrence but here the fundamental needs of wildlife and Man are identical. With a little care, our waterways can support both.

• *Colour pictures—page 60*

NATIONAL ANGLING

ENGLAND played host to 20 European angling nations in 1981 when the prestigious World Coarse Fishing Championships came to the banks of the Warwickshire Avon at Luddington, near historic Stratford.

The event tended to dominate the year's match-fishing calendar in terms of Press and TV attention but the four Divisional Championships organised for affiliated clubs and associations by the National Federation of Anglers are still the main attractions in each summer and autumn competitions programme.

Support for these championships remains strong with 303 teams of 12 participating in the 1981 series, 29 more than in the previous year—chiefly in entries for Division Four which has grown from 34 teams when inaugurated in 1978 to 80 in 1981.

Honour and glory and the chance to gain promotion to a higher division are the main reasons given by the hundreds trekking to the annual fixtures. But the opportunity to take a big win off the angling bookies in attendance also plays a part!

The Angler's Mail Annual NFA Championship Table shows winning teams and top individual performers from the start in 1906 to 1981, the latest to hand when this edition of the Annual was prepared for press. Ten teams are promoted to a higher division and 10 relegated each year, with Division One beckoning as the premier sector.

JOHN INGHAM

Go out and enjoy yourselves, advised CALPAC's National Championship team manager Peter Young at the assembly for the 1981 Division One event on the River Ancholme, Lincolnshire. Team member Dave Steer took the hint and won an enjoyable share of individual glory by taking the country's premier individual title with this 21 lb. 3 oz. bag of bream.

The mock scowl put on by Bill Knott, the angling bookmaker from Cornwall tells the story. He is parting with a £2,400 cheque to Bob Clampitt, a member of the Leatherhead team in the 1981 NFA Division Three event. Bob's 18 lb. 10½ oz. included four carp from the Oxford Canal and won him the individual title and the cash from bookie Bill.

LUTON matchman David Sayce rose at the crack of dawn to travel north for the 1981 Division Two National on the Leeds-Liverpool Canal at Liverpool. He was so tired during the match he could scarcely keep his eyes open but stayed awake long enough to net 16 lb. 15 oz. of tench to win the individual title.

We are the champions! Those soccer-type salutes signal success for the Essex County team in the 1981 NFA Division One Championship.

CHAMPIONSHIPS

N.F.A DIVISIONAL CHAMPIONSHIPS

Date	Venue	Teams	Winners	Team weight lb	oz	dr	Individual highest weight	lb	oz	dr
1906	R. Thames, Pangbourne	7	Boston	17	8	4	F. Beales (Boston)	4	11	0
1907	R. Witham, Kirkstead	13	Sheffield Amal.	21	12	12	A. Croft (Sheffield)	7	1	8
1908	North Level Drain, Tydd	13	Sheffield & Dist.	18	6	0	J. Mason (Sheffield)	12	2	0
1909	The Dyke, Newark, Notts.	18	Leeds Amal.	7	5	4	J. H. R. Bazley (Leeds)	2	2	8
1910	R. Derwent, Hutton's Ambo	17	Leeds Amal.	5	8	12	A. Blackman (Hull)	2	13	8
1911	R. Severn, Kimpsey	19	Sheffield Amal	53	6	0	W. Lowe (Sheffield)	13	4	0
1912	R. Ouse, Ely	20	Boston	25	9	0	G. Beales (Boston)	6	11	12
1913	R. Dee, Chester	22	Nottingham	2	15	0	W. Gough (Nottingham)	1	14	8
1914	R. Trent, Willington	20	Leeds Amal.	20	14	8	A. Skerratt (Derby)	6	15	12
1919	R. Ancholme, Brigg	24	Boston	20	0	8	T. Hill (Derby)	7	7	0
1920	R. Weaver, Hartford	29	County Palatine	12	4	0	R. Barlow (Hull)	3	1	0
1921	R. Trent, Burton Joyce	32	Derby	10	1	0	J. Wakesfield (Derby)	6	2	12
1922	R. Witham, Kirkstead	38	Lincoln	10	5	12	B. Hobday (Lincoln)	3	5	8
1923	R. Soar, Kegworth	41	County Palatine	18	11	0	J. W. Couldwell (Sheffield)	5	15	8
1924	R. Glen, Pinchbeck, Lincs.	43	Castleford & Dist.	28	0	8	W. T. Willcocks (London)	21	8	8
1925	R. Severn, Worcester	46	Long Eaton	5	10	8	G. Allen (Provincial)	3	8	12
1926	R. Ouse, Naburn, Yorks.	47	Lincoln	23	11	9	A. Fletcher (Boston)	7	1	0
1927	Middle Level Drain, Kings Lynn, Norfolk	47	Grimsby & Dist.	44	5	12	J. H. R. Bazley (Leeds)	16	5	8
1928	R. Severn, Tewkesbury, Glos.	44	Leeds & Dist.	13	2	13	W. Tetley (Leeds)	3	13	3
1929	R. Witham, Kirkstead, Lincs.	44	Boston	50	4	0	J. Sykes (Boston)	10	15	0
1930	R. Soar, Kegworth, Derby	51	Sheffield Amal.	43	10	0	C. Muddimer (Leicester)	15	6	0
1931	South Forty Foot Drain	48	Hull Amal.	27	9	8	O. Daddy (Hull)	19	9	8
1932	R. Soar, Kegworth, Derby	47	Loughborough	24	15	0	H. Sallis (Long Eaton)	5	9	4
1933	R. Great Ouse, Olney, Bucks.	48	Sheffield & Dist.	33	6	4	Edgar Dabill (Sheffield)	13	15	9
1934	R. Thames, Abingdon, Berks.	54	Sheffield Amal.	14	3	11	H. Smith (Sheffield)	4	14	4
1935	R. Witham, Kirkstead, Lincs.	50	Lincoln	43	13	2	A. Kellett (Doncaster)	18	6	15
1936	R. Thurne, Potter Heighham	53	Lincoln	74	5	15	A. E. Bryant (Buckingham)	35	1	0
1937	Gloucester Canal	56	Groves & Whitnall	23	15	6	H. Jones (Co. Palatine)	9	9	9
1938	R. Great Ouse, Harrold	62	Hull & Dist.	38	12	7	G. Bright (Bristol)	21	13	8
1945	R. Trent, Newark, Notts.	57	Worksop	75	2	5	M. T. Cotteril (Worksop)	16	1	7
1946	R. Witham, Langrick, Notts.	66	Hull	57	0	12	G. Laybourne (York)	12	12	8
1947	R. Witham, Kirkstead, Lincs.	70	Worksop	57	8	4	W. Edwards (Rotherham)	9	4	8
1948	R. Huntspill, Somerset	72	Leeds Amal.	23	14	4	W. Thompson, (Leeds)	14	9	12
1949	R. Thurne, Potter Heigham	77	Leeds Amal.	49	3	4	R. Woodhall (Whit. Reans)	15	6	8
1950	R. Nene, Peterborough	81	Peterborough	62	5	12	W. Rockley (Peterborough)	15	4	0
1951	R. Witham, Kirkstead, Lincs.	82	Doncaster	93	5	0	S. Buxton (Doncaster)	20	13	4
1952	R. Severn, Bridgnorth, Salop	88	Leeds Amal.	135	5	0	H. Seed (Leeds)	33	5	4
1953	R. Nene, Peterborough	92	Lincoln	72	5	0	N. N. Hazelwood (Cmb.)	27	14	0
1954	R. Trent, Gunthorpe, Notts.	98	Hull Angling Pres.	68	13	1	R. Lye (Notts. Fed.)	15	1	12
1955	R. Huntspill, Bridgewater, Som.	99	Sheffield Amal.	136	15	4	J. Carr (Sheffield Amal.)	68	2	4
1956	R. Witham, Kirkstead, Lincs.	94	Coventry & Dist.	86	4	4	C. R. Lusby (Lincoln)	25	8	0
1957	R. Severn, Bridgnorth, Salop	96	Notts. A.A.	22	8	1	H. Storey (Notts. A.A.)	7	12	8
1958	R. Welland, Spalding, Lincs.	98	Coventry A.A.	59	15	4	W. Hughes (Northern Anglers)	24	3	0
1959	R. Nene, Peterborough	100	Bedford A.C.	86	1	4	J. Sharpe (Bedford)	57	8	8
1960	Rs. Ante, Bure, Thurne, Nflk.	101	King's Lynn A.A.	81	15	1	K. Smith (Norwich)	50	14	8
1961	R. Trent, Nottingham	103	Coventry A.A.	77	6	12	J. Blakey (Saltaire)	23	12	12
1962	R. Welland, Spalding, Lins.	103	Lincoln	56	2	12	V. A. Baker (Derby Railway)	13	11	0
1963	Gloucester Canal	105	Northampton Nene A.C.	19	11	2	R. Sims (N. Som. & West Wilts.)	14	15	2
1964	R. Severn, Worcester	107	Kidderminster	50	13	2	G. Burch (Essex County)	32	3	0
1965	R. Huntspill, Somerset	110	Rugby Federation	93	7	8	D. Burr (Rugby)	76	9	0
1966	R. Witham, Lincs.	108	Boston	75	1	4	R. Jarvis (Boston)	29	1	8
1967	Relief Channel, Norfolk	111	Derby Railway	83	4	4	E. Townsin (Cambridge F.P.)	40	6	8
1968	Rs. Ante, Bure, Thurne, Nflk.	112	Leighton Buzzard	74	0	8	D. Groom (Leighton Buzzard)	36	6	0
1969	R. Trent, Nottingham	114	Stoke	32	8	2	R. Else (Lincoln)	9	7	3
1970	Middle Level Drain	113	Cambridge FPS	97	2	0	B. Lakey (Cambridge)	35	4	8
1971	R. Severn, Stourport	116	Leicester	124	8	8	R. Harris (Peterborough)	40	5	0

Continued next page

N.F.A DIVISIONAL CHAMPIONSHIPS

Continued from previous page

Date / Venue	Teams	Winners	Team weight lb	oz	dr	Team points	Individual highest weight	lb	oz	dr
1972 Div. 1: Bristol Avon	79	Birmingham A.A.	51	1	12	248	P. Coles (Leicester)	33	8	0
Div 2: R. Welland	81	Coleshill, Warwks.	72	15	8	216	J. Hart (Whittlesey) Cambs.)	54	14	8
1973 Div: 1 R. Witham	80	Grimsby A.S.A.	92	10	4	717	A. Wright (Derby Rly. Inst.)	41	10	8
Div. 2: Gt. Ouse Relief Channel	92	Leigh & Dist. (Lancs.)	76	6	8	826	J. Wilkinson (Elthorne A.S., Hanwell)	43	1	8
1974 Div. 1: R. Welland	80	Leicester A.S.	25	9	4	733	P. Anderson (Cambridge F.P.A.S.)	40	2	8
Div. 2: Avon (Warwks.)	85	Stockport Fed.	71	0	8	1161	C. Hibbs (Leigh Miners)	47	3	8
1975 Div. 1: R. Nene	79	Birmingham A.A.	43	15	12	814	M. Hoad-Reddick (Rotherham U.A.F.)	63	7	0
Div. 2: R. Trent	71	Long Eaton Victoria A.S., Nottingham	60	6	4	735	A. Webber (Wigan)	16	2	8
Div. 3: R. Welland	42	Crawley A.S., Sussex	18	9	0	394	J. Garrett (GEC Marconi, Chelmsford)	24	8	0
1976 Div. 1: R. Trent	79	Birmingham A.A.	53	14	4	776	N. Wells (Newark)	28	0	8
Div. 2: R. Witham	76	Izaak Walton (Preston) A.S.	34	14	8	783	P. Marks (Exeter)	12	11	8
Div. 3: R. Huntspill, South and King's Sedgemoor Drains	80	London A.A.	47	6	4	693	D. Knox (Cheadle)	38	9	12
1977 Div. 1: R. Welland	77	Coventry A.A.	25	15	4	755	R. Foster (Rotherham)	39	10	4
Div. 2: Grt. Ouse	72	Huntingdon A.S.	34	10	12	687	S. Yeomans (Reading)	24	3	0
Div. 3: R. Trent	90	Stratford upon Avon A.A.	30	9	0	881	C. Robinson (Barnet)	18	4	8
1978 Div. 1: Bristol Avon	79	Coleshill & Dist. A.S.	84	11	8	790	D. Harris (Bradford City)	48	13	0
R. Trent	78	Nottingham A.A.	36	13	4	806	I. Carrier (Long Eaton)	10	5	8
Div. 3: R. Witham	74	Bathampton A.A.	33	13	4	712	L. Constable (Chatteris)	29	8	8
Div. 4: R. Huntspill South & King's Sedgemoor Drains	34	Swindon Talisman A.C.	30	1	0	353	B. Shepherd (Ramsey & Dist. A.C.)	56	2	0
1979 Div. 1: Gt. Ouse and R. Cam	80	Barnsley	10	15	4	700	M. Cullen (Oxford & Dist.)	11	8	0
Div. 2: R. Witham	80	Bathampton A.A.	32	2	0	746	S. White (Leek & Morelands)	11	13	0
Div. 3: R. Welland and Coronation Channel	73	Swindon Talisman A.C.	56	1	8	769	P. Deacon (Wellingborough & Dist)	17	5	0
Div. 4: R. Trent	56	Marazion A.C.	79	12	8	571	G. Salisbury (Marazion A.C.)	34	6	0
1980 Div. 1: R. Trent	80	Nottingham Fed.	93	5	12	883	P. Burrell (Essex County)	27	8	0
Div. 2: R. Witham	74	Oundle	33	10	8	735	D. Green (Boston)	46	0	0
Div. 3: R. Ancholme	68	Wisbech	42	1	0	664	A. Kelly (Kidsgrove)	13	1	8
Div. 4: Yorks. Ouse	52	Telford (Salop)	7	13	12	461	D. Hall (Stoke)	6	10	8
1981 Div. 1: R. Ancholme	79	Essex County	19	7	0	714	D. Steer (CALPAC)	21	3	0
Div. 2: Leeds/Liverpool Canal	73	Southport D.A.A.	52	3	4	687	D. Sayce (Luton)	16	15	0
Div. 3: Oxford Canal	71	North Staffs.	23	15	8	741	B. Clampitt (Leatherhead)	18	10	8
Div. 4: R. Thames	80	Lamb A.C.	53	4	4	764	P. Hamlyn (Maidstone Victory)	20	0	8

CAPTAIN MORGAN CUP

THE Captain Morgan Cup competition is match angling's equivalent of soccer's FA Cup. Television cameras filmed the event for the first time in 1981 and the winning Dorking team did the programme justice by taking a record weight of 834 lb.

That set a new weight record for a 12-man team and pushed Leeds into the losers' seats by more than 200 lb. Luckless Leeds, who mustered 608 lb. muffed their chances after being misled by a practise session on the day before the final on Ulster's River Bann.

Dorking opted for the roach pole instead of the waggler float methods chosed by Leeds and took the top three individual weights . . . Steve Gardener 103 lb., skipper Ken Collings just 2½ ounces less and Geoff Vallance 94½ lb.

N.F.A LADIES NATIONAL CHAMPIONSHIPS

TEENAGER Claire Legge added yet another trophy to her collection of angling awards when she won the 1981 NFA Ladies National Championship on South Cerney's Ashton Keynes gravel pit. Before winning this Craddock-sponsored event, Claire, 16, had already made angling history by becoming the first girl to skipper Birmingham AA's Junior National team.

● Special feature, page 69.

1981 WORLD CHAMPIONSHIPS

Give us a kiss! Word champion Dave Thomas collects a congratulatory smacker from his wife, Avis, a former Ladies National Champion.

LEEDS postal worker Dave Thomas scored a unique double when he became England's fourth individual world champion on the River Avon at Luddington, near Stratford, Warwickshire, in September 1981.

He was the first to win the world title AND make top weight in the teams championship, which is held on the day before the individual contest.

Dave, who was the first *Angler's Mail* Matchman of the Year in 1978, put just over 10 lb. of chub on the scales for top weight in the teams match. On the following day, when the River Avon was badly coloured and out of form due to flood water, he took two chub and a roach for the world crown with 2 lb. 9 oz.

Both catches were made on float-fished bronze maggots, the bait which has made Dave a famous name among match anglers.

The only other English anglers to win the world title are Billy Lane, Robin Harris and Ian Heaps—with a gap of six years between each win.

Gotcha! One of the fish which helped towards Dave's top individual weight in the teams match.

ANGLING CHAMPIONSHIPS

Cheers! A partisan crowd gathers behind Dave Thomas on the banks of the Warwickshire Avon as he moves towards a world individual title. Each of the three fish he landed brought a loud cheer from his loyal fans.

France won the 1981 World Teams Championship for the eleventh time in the 25 years history of these contests. Three of their wins were scored between 1978 and 1981.

England were forced into second place for the second successive year, even though their host nation status gave them the choice of venue. But the French admitted after the match they could not have defeated England if the river levels had been normal.

Wales competed for the first time and came a creditable third. Scotland finished twelfth and Ireland seventeenth in the 20-teams line-up.

● *Exclusive colour pictures, page 57*

COLIN MITCHELL

Dave Thomas (below) plays another fish towards his waiting landing net in the 1981 World Championships on the Warwickshire Avon.

France's top scorer in the teams match was Jean Pierre Fougeat, a former world individual champion. He is pictured dealing with another roach.

French coach Fortune Jacquelin holds the World trophy. Looking on are team members and England men Dave Thomas, Kevin Ashurst and Max Winters (left).

NATIONAL JUNIOR CHAMPIONSHIP

THERE'S no room for male chauvinism in match fishing, as the Northern AA showed when Amanda Collier and Catherine Shirley helped them to crush the local lads from Leeds ASA into second place in the 1981 NFA Junior National Championship on the Leeds-Liverpool Canal.

Date	Venue	Teams	Winners	Team weight lb	oz	dr	Team points	Individual highest weight	lb	oz	dr
1978	Leeds-Liverpool Canal	56	Stockport & Dist.	21	1	4	611	A. Hunt (Coventry)	8	4	0
1979	Warwickshire Avon	51	Bristol and West	33	2	8	491	G. Bennett (B'ham)	17	10	0
1980	R. Trent	70	Leicester A.S.	27	2	12	708	P. Matthews (Newark)	16	10	0
1981	Leeds-Liverpool Canal	60	Northern A.A.	13	0	0	655	M. Church (Long Eaton Vic.)	5	8	4

Angler's Mail — Leisure Sport

BRITISH JUNIOR CHAMPIONSHIPS

Nottingham youngster Michael Church came close to an incredible double in his 1981 match season when only a week after winning the NFA Junior National he won through to the finals of the new Angler's Mail—Leisure Sport British Junior Championships . . . but could manage only seventh place on the day.

Michael, 15, a member of Long Eaton Victoria club, took a bag of small carp for 7 lb. 13 oz. in Leisure Sport's Aldermaston Pit, near Reading, Berkshire.

First winner of the new Championships was Richard Fox, from Hornchurch, Essex, with 17 lb. 11 oz. of carp, the species which gained him a place in the final when he landed top weight of 7 lb. 6½ oz. in the preliminary heat at Stanford-le-Hope pit, Essex.

Angler's Mail staff reporter Beverly Adams presents the winner's trophy to the first British Junior Champion, Richard Fox of Hornchurch.

Michael Church receives his awards in the NFA Junior National from Federation President Joe Betteridge.

HOLIDAY SHORE SPOTS

MENAI STRAIT, WALES

The twelve-mile Menai Straits offer shore-fishing from rocks and sand for a large number of different fish from the humble dab to big bass.

Local knowledge plays a large part in making catches because the narrow Strait, which separates mainland Wales from the island of Anglesey, can create an extremely strong tide race.

Among the most popular short marks is the rocky section on the Anglesey side between Menai and Britannia Bridge, although tackle losses can be heavy due to the snaggy bottom. But for those with the necessary skill and perseverance, there can be pollack, bass, conger and the occasional big "flattie".

The best chance of taking quality plaice and flounders is from farther along the Straits at Port Dinorwic. The fishing at Foryd Bay is also noted for "flatties", as is the Caernarfon area.

Pollack, coalfish and "flatties" are taken regularly from the opposite end of the Strait, near Bangor. One of the best marks is near the boathouse situated midway between Bangor Pier and Menai Road Bridge.

Menai Strait has one other important asset to offer—fresh bait. This is an excellent area for collecting peeler crab and there are plenty of worm beds. The soft sand near to Bangor Pier is a well-known lugworm area and although several places along the shore do hold ragworm they tend to be on the small side and time spent travelling to nearby Lleiniog may be worthwhile.

There are fishing tackle shops in Menai village and at Caernarfon. A stop at the Tackle Box, Colwyn Bay, can produce some sound advice.

WHITSAND BAY TO RAME HEAD, CORNWALL

The surf beaches and headlands along the wild stretch of coast embracing Whitsand Bay to Rame Head in South East Cornwall is a shore fisherman's paradise.

Bass are the principal quarry but due to considerable gill-netting activity on the coast and offshore the numbers of fish are nothing like they were. Large specimens are still about and recent catches at Seaton Beach include fish of 13 lb 2 oz and 11½ lb, both falling to big fish-baits. Other recommended centres for bass include nearby Portwrinkle, Tregantle and Polhawn.

The best fishing can be expected at night on a rising tide, just after a big southerly blow. From the beaches a cast of at least 100 yards is needed to reach behind the third breaker, where larger fish are generally found.

Work from the rocky outcrops—the Grotto at Ffeathy is a good example, and really deep water can be reached with only a moderate cast.

Terminal rigs can be a single-hook leger or a two-hook paternoster baited with live sandeel or, if this is not available, neatly-cut strips of squid or fresh mackerel. King ragworm can be dug at nearby Jupiter Point or Torpoint Balast Pond and is also a worthwhile bait.

In winter, large pollack come close to the Grotto where fish in the 14 lb class have been spotted. Spinning with small artificials and to a lesser extent metal lures, is the best means of attracting the pollack.

Beaches on either side of the rocky spit can be fished for flounder and other types of flatfish, including turbot, but these generally weigh

ADMIRALTY PIER, DOVER

Admiralty Pier, Dover, is over 4,000 feet long and offers an angler a wide selection of fish throughout the year. It is always open for angling and there is no charge.

Car parking can be difficult in summer months close to the pier entrance but there are several streets and car parks within a reasonable walking distance.

The first section of the pier is where the large majority of flounders, dabs and plaice are caught due to the bottom being sandy for the most part. Large numbers of mackerel are landed in July and August.

The second half of the pier is renowned for all-round good fishing for bass in summer and cod in winter.

The seabed consists of rocks, weed and some areas of sand and shingle. Keep tackle losses to a minimum by avoiding fishing close to the wall, especially during the tide run.

Mullet to 5 lb. are taken on bread bait from late June to early October

little more than 3 lb.

Species in the Portwrinkle area during winter are coalfish and whiting, taken on thin strips of squid or bunched worm offered on leger tackle.

Rame Head is at the east end of the bay and is one of the most prominent headlands in the English Channel with a series of deep gullies infested with thick kelp weed which shelter very big wrasse.

The largest cleft is to the left of the Head and reached by a steep path followed by a 30 ft climb down an eroded cliff face. The gully holds 20 ft of water at low tide.

Ballan wrasse hide under the overhangs of rock and a long-handled landing net is essential as at high tide the water is still five feet below the lowest accessible ledge.

Big conger also hole up in Rame's underwater caverns. When darkness sets in they feed freely on mackerel or squid baits but it is essential to find a spot where a big eel can be safely gaffed ashore. For that reason it is best to arrive on the rocks an hour before the light goes.

Whitsand Bay is on Ordnance Survey sheet No. 201, 1.50,000 series.

on the rising tides and black bream, huss, pouting, pollack, conger and other species are landed throughout the summer season.

Bait supplies are limited in Dover during winter months and especially September, October and November when major pier and boat festivals are taking place, so bait should be ordered well in advance to avoid problems.

The tide race at the Admiralty Pier is very strong during spring tides and fishing is almost impossible from the extension for 1½ hours after. On the lower neap tides the run can be fished right through, using anchor weights, when sport can be very productive for cod on these tides in winter.

Bait suppliers: Bill's Bait & Tackle, 130 Snargate Street, (Dover 204542); D. J. Brazil, Angler's Den, 162 Snargate Street (Dover 201457); Dover Tackle Shop, 146 Snargate Street; (Dover 203742).

FILEY BRIGG

East Yorkshire's rock mark known as Filey Brigg is a reef about a mile long which extends seawards, north of Filey Bay. Geologically, it is described as a corraline oolite ridge topped with boulder clay.

There are two approaches to Filey Brigg. The longest walk is to set off on foot from the coble landing and take the beach route to reach the concrete path on the south side of the Brigg. But this path is covered by the sea from about half-tide up until half-ebb.

The most convenient way to approach the area is to drive to the extensive cliff top car park and then walk a short distance over the cliff top to the north side of the Brigg, descending to the rock ledges by way of the vertical iron escape ladder.

Alternatively, keep to the cliffs until they slope down gradually on to the Brigg. This route is apt to be very "sticky" in wet weather.

The Brigg is famous for its kelp-bed fishing for "native" or "red" codling, which can be taken the whole year round. Soft or peeler crab is the cod bait supreme and it is necessary to fish with what is known locally as a "rotten bottom" terminal rig, with the sinker secured by a weak link of line. This is because continual snagging is an accepted part of rock-mark kelp angling.

In high summer, mackerel fishing from the Brigg can be quite fantastic, but conversely, some years see a complete absence of these fish. Light spinning tackle will take them in good numbers when they are shoaling around the flat rock ledges (or "scaurs" as they are known locally). Floatfishing with fish strips or lasks of a freshly caught mackerel is also a deadly method. But small coalfish (known in the North-East as billet) are apt to prove a bait-grabbing nuisance.

Where it is possible to cast on to flat snag-free sand—mostly on the Filey (south) side—some good plaice and dabs can be taken with the chance of an occasional bass.

Lugworms can be dug at various locations along the flat and gently shelving beaches on the Filey side of the Brigg and there are also extensive colonies of razorfish which are exposed on the big spring tides at low water, especially just seawards of the coble landing.

A word of warning to vistors unfamiliar with rock kelp-mark fishing— wear suitably studded footwear to give a secure grip on the green weed. Watch the line of retreat when fishing at the extreme end of the Brigg on a rising tide and give the high ledge marks a wide berth in times of heavy rainfall as the grass tracks to these become rather like a water chute.

Local tackle dealer and bait supplier—R. Dale, Hope Street, Filey.

INLAND HOLIDAY SPOTS

WESSEX

River Huntspill, Somerset

Location: Three main access points—(1) From A38 road bridge approximately three miles from Highbridge, travelling towards Bridgwater; (2) For Wollavington Bridge, turn left in Highbridge on to B3139 Wedmore Road and follow for about 1½ miles then take B3141, right-turn signposted East Huntspill and Basin Bridge. Follow this road for approximately three miles to Wollavington Bridge over the Huntspill. This is the second river bridge—the first river bridge crosses the River Brue. (3) For Gold Corner, follow as for Wollavington Bridge, but one mile after crossing River Brue take a left-turn, signposted Edington Burtle situated on a sharp right-hand bend. Follow this for one mile to a T-junction then turn right at signpost for Gold Corner. Follow this lane to bridge over River Huntspill where River Cripps and South Drain enter.

Parking: areas at all bridges.

Day, monthly and yearly permits issued by Bridgwater AA., obtainable from all tackle shops in area or from pumphouse cottage at Gold Corner.

This is a vast man-made drain some 80 ft wide in places with normally only a slight flow. Contains big shoals of bream from 2½ lb to 6 lb with roach, perch, eels and skimmers.

Legering with worm or worm-pinkie cocktail over groundbait laced with squatts is favoured method, although waggler-fished caster two rodlengths out is best for roach and skimmers.

Christchurch Harbour

Location: Christchurch, Dorset

Parking: Various areas in the vicinity of harbour.

Permits: Harbour tickets £1 day, £5.75 season, from Davis Tackle, Bargates, Christchurch; or Nimrod Tackle, Castle Parade, Iford, Bournemouth.

Description: From where the Avon and the Stour meet to the sea, good mullet fishing and coarse fish depending on tides. Varied and interesting fishing controlled by Christchurch AC.

Royalty Fishery, Hampshire Avon.

Location: Christchurch, Dorset.

Permits: Full details should be obtained from Davis Tackle, Bargates, Christchurch. There are many types of tickets and prices vary depending on which part of the fishery is selected.

Description: Typical stretch of the Hampshire Avon containing most species. Approx. one mile, in most cases double bank, and two weirs. Probably the most famous fishery in the country with plenty of barbel well into double-figures and some good chub, roach and dace, also occasional good bream.

ANGLIAN

Tidal River Yare, Norfolk

From south-east Norwich head over Trowse Bridge spanning the River Yare and take first turn on left down Whitlingham Lane. One and a half miles farther on, the river can be seen on left, alongside lane. Access starts at a dyke which joins mainstream on wide bend and continues down-river until marshes restrict access.

Parking on verge between river and lane and in large parking area set back on right of lane.

All fishing on Norfolk's tidal waterways is free provided access is available.

This stretch is wide and easy to fish, with deep water close in, affording good mixed catches of roach, bream and hybrids. Fishes well at night during summer but is a better daytime winter fishery when some reasonable pike can be expected. Mostly float-fishing with maggots and casters just tripping the bottom, but better catches of bream fall to the lead in midstream.

THAMES

King's Weir Fishery, Wormley, Herts

Take A10 from London and at Broxbourne turn right into Station Road. Cross railway bridge and continue for half-mile, then turn right, signposted Old Nazeing Road, and after 100 yards turn left into Green Lane. At end of road continue down track and park where indicated.

Flood Relief Channel is on left, the lake is straight ahead and river is to the right of the lake.

Day tickets are available for the lake and Relief Channel only, price 50p. Season tickets available for river, lake, and channel, £15 for adults and £10 for juniors and OAPs, Guest tickets for river are available to full season-ticket holders price £1 at discretion of fishery manager.

The fishery consists of half-mile of old River Lea, both banks, three-quarters-mile of the Flood Relief Channel, both banks, and three-quarters-mile of bank of Langridge Lake.

The focal point is King's Weir itself, famous for its barbel and chub fishing. The weir pool may be fished from punts which are bookable and cost £5 per day.

The Flood Relief Channel is well-stocked with bream and roach and the lake fishes well for tench, bream, roach and pike.

YORKSHIRE

River Ure, Ullshaw Bridge

Location: Proceed north via A1 to signs for Bedale. Pass through village, heading for Bedale. Pass through village, heading towards Leyburn. Take left turn for Harmby and look for Old Horn Inn at Spennithorne. Proceed to road junction, take right turn and park on grass verge in side lane opposite entry on left just before river bridge. Entry to fishery at Bridgewell is signposted.

Permits: Obtainable from Old Horn Inn, Spennithorne. Adults 70p and concessions for juveniles.

Description: This fishery is managed by Leeds and District ASA and caters for 20 rods. Good early season spot for trout. Big dace in plenty. Floatfished maggot is the best method but minnows are a menace in summer months. Superb grayling fishing towards the back end of the season.

SOUTHERN

West Hythe Gravel Pit, Kent

Location: Take A259 coast road from Hythe to Dymchurch. At Palmarsh there is a garage on right—adjacent to garage is entrance to pits.

Permits: £1 per day, available from bailiff. Bailiff's hut is just inside entrance.

Parking: Designated parking areas beside pit. Bailiff will clarify parking on arrival.

This is a large gravel pit, still being worked. Average depth about 15 to 20 feet but with a shallow arm with average depth of about 6 ft.

The pit holds perch, tench, bream, roach, pike, eels and carp. The perch and roach grow large and the carp have been taken to 20 lb-plus. Bream are not particularly large but plentiful in the 2 to 3 lb range.

Floatfishing in the marginal shelf will find roach and bream but distance legering with worms and casters is more effective for the bigger bream.

The gates are shut in the evening and not re-opened until the morning. Times are posted on a notice-board near the entrance. Night fishing is by arrangement with the bailiff.

SOUTH-WEST

Squabmoor Reservoir, Devon

From Exeter take the B3179 road for Woodbury, and through village to junction with B3180. Turn right, then after two miles to a junction. Look for Budleigh Salterton sign and continue along road for approx. one mile then turn left to East Budleigh Common. Reservoir on right-hand side, half-a-mile along. Car parking space near reservoir.

Permits available from SWWA South-West Water Authority which controls fishing. Day ticket £1.50, OAP's and juniors 75p. Season, adults £20, juniors £10. Day permits from Knowle Post Office; The Tackle Shop, Strand, Exmouth; and Exeter Angling Centre, City Arcade, Fore St., Exeter.

This is a man-made reservoir of around four acres, with shallows opposite the deep water dam wall. Fairly well lined with trees and bushes and stocked with trout, making the reservoir available for fishing all year round.

Float fishing and legering methods both take fish. Sweetcorn and bread are very successful for the carp.

SCOTLAND

Castle Loch, Lochmaben

Leave the A74 Carlisle to Glasgow road and Locherbie and take A709 towards Dumfries. About four miles along A709 is Lochmaben with Castle Loch right beside the road.

Alongside the loch on A709 is a large lay-by where many anglers park when fishing the east side of loch. The west shoreline is reached by going into Lochmaben and turning left on to B7020 where parking is on roadside.

To fish southern end of loch, proceed along B7020 until signs for Lochmaben Castle. Follow these signs up a lane then turn on to a rough track down to lakeside.

Permits available from Hallheaths Estate bailiff at his cottage alongside the lay-by on A709.

This is a large water with well-rushed verges offering depths of 13-18 ft. at two to three rodlengths. The best catches of fish are generally made where the bed runs out reasonably shallow then drops quite sharply. It is along here that the bream do their patrolling.

Loch Maben is noted as the best bream fishing in Scotland with treble-figure catches not too uncommon.

Take a lot of groundbait as the bream shoals are generally large. The fish are everywhere but night fishing by the effluent treatment works alongside the A709 has proved the most effective. Loch also holds good roach, hybrids, tench and carp.

HOLIDAY CENTRES

Two anglers set out for a day's fishing with Blenheim Palace dominating the background.

BLENHEIM FOR STATELY

Blenheim Palace, home of the Churchill family, attracts many thousands of visitors every year but not only tourists flock to this stately home set in the rolling Oxfordshire countryside . . . hundreds of anglers journey to Blenheim Lake to sample some of the best stillwater fishing in the country.

Whether the quarry is tench, pike or bream this lake can turn up some spectactular catches in the shadow of one of the most famous and best-loved stately homes of England, which the family can tour while Dad enjoys the fishing.

Blenheim is just over an hour's drive from the outskirts of London, via the A40 and M40. Oxford city traffic congestion is avoided by following the ring-road when the signs for Woodstock and Blenheim are soon sighted.

The imposing sandstone-coloured palace is an awe-inspiring building but for those who have their sights set on the fishing the huge landscaped lake is an even better prospect.

The massive expanse of water is set perfectly in the gently rolling landscape only a short walk from the carefully-tended palace gardens.

A walk down the steeply-shelving bank leads to the covered boathouse where a number of well-scrubbed punts lie at moorings. These craft are big and ideal for angling but can be a little ungainly, especially when a cross-wind is blowing.

Blenheim lake has built up something of a big fish reputation over the last decade. According to Oxfordshire expert Peter Stone, it is not uncommon to net 50 lb. of tench in a session.

"The trick is to find the deeper holes in the lake," he advises. "These tend to be in the middle."

"Locating between eight and ten feet of water means being in with a chance of contacting the tench, which can be in up to 5 lb. Not all the fish grow that big but it should be possible to catch a boatload in the 3 lb. range".

Anglers fishing Blenheim for the first time can be a little bewildered by the size of the water. The left-hand side of the lake, looking from the palace bank, narrows into a funnel with the banks lined with thick reeds.

Viewed from the other way the lake spreads out and one arm disappears out of sight. It's a long row in the palace punts to those areas but the back-breaking effort can pay dividends. For it is here that some of the lake's breathtaking catches of tench have been made in recent years. Regulars, like Peter, nearly always fish the water on the float, with most of the popular baits attracting fish.

The thick reeds which surround Blenheim lake make ideal cover.